D0789953

Shameless Exploitation

IN PURSUIT OF
THE COMMON GOOD

ALSO BY

PAUL NEWMAN

AND A. E. HOTCHNER

The Hole in the Wall Gang Cookbook:
   Kid-Friendly Recipes for Families to Make Together

Newman's Own Cookbook

NAN A. TALESE

Doubleday

new york ・ london
toronto ・ sydney
auckland

Shameless Exploitation

IN PURSUIT OF
THE COMMON GOOD

Paul Newman
and
A. E. Hotchner

PUBLISHED BY NAN A. TALESE

AN IMPRINT OF DOUBLEDAY

a division of Random House, Inc.

1745 Broadway, New York, NY 10019

DOUBLEDAY is a registered trademark of Random House, Inc.

BOOK DESIGN BY DEBORAH KERNER /

DANCING BEARS DESIGN

Library of Congress Cataloging-in-Publication Data

Newman, Paul, 1925–

Shameless exploitation in pursuit of the common good / Paul
Newman and A. E. Hotchner.— 1st ed.

p.   cm.

1. Newman's Own (Firm)   2. Camps—organizations—United
States. 3. Social responsibility of business—United States.

4. Human ecology—United States.   I. Hotchner, A. E.   II. Title.

HD9330.S26N496 2003

338.7'66458'092273—dc22

[B]   2003059665

We thank all the many people who have written letters to us in
appreciation of Newman's Own over the years, in particular those whose
letters are included in these pages.

ISBN 0-385-50802-6

Copyright © 2003 The Association of the Hole in the Wall Gang
Camps and A. E. Hotchner

All Rights Reserved

PRINTED IN THE UNITED STATES OF AMERICA

December 2003

First Edition

1   3   5   7   9   10   8   6   4   2

We dedicate this book to

DR. ANNE DYSON and ALICE TRILLIN,

two remarkable women who are sorely missed

by the Hole in the Wall Gang

CONTENTS

FOREWORD

Sometimes you get what you want but it ain't what you expected. Newman's Own was supposed to be a tiny boutique operation—parchment labels on elegant wine bottles of antique glass. We expected train wrecks along the way and got, instead, one astonishment followed by another astonishment followed by another. We flourished like weeds in the garden of Wishbone, like silver in the vaults of finance. A lot of the time we thought we were in first gear we were really in reverse, but it didn't seem to make any difference. We anticipated sales of $1,200 a year and a loss, despite our gambling winnings, of $6,000. But in these twenty years we have earned over $150 million, which we've given to countless charities. How to account for this massive success? Pure luck? Transcendental meditation? Machiavellian manipulation? Aerodynamics? High colonics?

We haven't the slightest idea.

PL & AE

PART ONE

Shameless Exploitation

In the queer mess of human destiny the determining factor is Luck. For every important place in life there are many men of fairly equal capacities. Among them Luck divides who shall accomplish the great work, who shall be crowned with laurel, and who shall fall back in obscurity and silence.

—WILLIAM E. WOODWARD

CHAPTER

1

It is December 1980, a week before Christmas, Westport, Connecticut, a blanket of snow on the ground, wood smoke from fireplaces redolent in the air, tree lights festooning the houses, a pervasive Yuletide lilt, but we are laboring in the subterranean space beneath Paul's converted barn, an area that had once been a stable for farm horses. There is a bucket filled with ice-blanketed Budweisers and an array of bottles of olive oil, vinegar, mustard, condiments, and so forth. There is also an empty tub and a collection of old bottles dating back to Revolutionary times by their appearance, bottles of various shapes and sizes that had been somewhat sanitized for this occasion.

Paul Newman, known to his friends as ol' PL or Calezzo de Wesso (Bonehead), had asked his buddy A. E. Hotchner (Hotch), sometimes called Sawtooth, to help him with a Christmas project that he was assembling in this basement, which wasn't a basement in the usual sense. There were crusty stones, a dirt floor, crumbling cement, and overhead timbers covered with active cobwebs. Also three long since vacated horse stalls, but the unmistakable aroma of horses remained. There were desiccated manure fragments here and there, and there was evidence that certain field animals were still occupying the premises. A very picturesque place in which to mix salad dressing.

The project was to mix up a batch of PL's salad dressing in the washtub and fill all those old wine bottles using the assembled funnels and corks and labels, and on Christmas Eve our collective families would go around the neighborhood singing carols and distributing these gift bottles of PL's dressing.

PL was very proud of his salad dressing, and this was the apotheosis of his salad days. Over the years, even in four-star restaurants, PL had been rejecting the house dressings and concocting his own. Captains, maître d's, and sometimes the restaurant owner would scurry around to assemble Paul's ingredients while neighboring diners gawked in disbelief. When we first ate at Elaine's, one of New York's popular restaurants, several waiters and Elaine herself gathered round as Paul blended and tasted the brew he made from the ingredients brought to him from the kitchen. This scene had been repeated in such varied eateries as a Greek diner, at a wedding party, in an outdoor restaurant, on the island of Eleuthera, and in snazzy restaurants from coast to coast. When his kids went off to school, Paul would fill a couple of bottles of dressing for them to take along. On one occasion, when the restaurant mistakenly served the salad with its own dressing, Paul took the salad to the men's room, washed off the dressing, dried it with paper towels, and, after returning to the table, anointed it with his own, which he concocted with ingredients brought to him from the kitchen.

At that time, almost all dressings, especially the mass-market ones, contained sugar, artificial coloring, chemical preservatives, gums, and God knows what. So Paul really started to make his own dressing not just as a taste preference, but also as a defense against those insufferable artificial additives.

That evening the basement operation seemed to go on forever. We had never tried to mix a vat of salad dressing, let alone pound a 1925 syrup cork into an 1895 vinegar bottle, especially after a few beers. Sometimes the mallet would smack the cork, and sometimes it nailed our thumbs. Paul carefully measured amounts of olive oil and vinegar, for he had no feel yet for dealing with a quantity like this, which, he decided, required six boxes of black pepper.

He was almost crazed as he stirred the dressing with the wooden paddle. There's a river that runs alongside his house, and the paddle most certainly came from his canoe. It was his notion that the olive oil and vinegar had a sort of hygienic effect so that one didn't have to wash anything thoroughly. That aside, he was highly critical of Hotch's paddle technique. The motion, he insisted, had to have an even, smooth rhythm that would not create frothing. But Hotch couldn't get the hang of it. "You've got to go with the paddle," Paul said. "Don't pull it straight toward you, waffle it, gyrate it, go with the paddle." Hotch said he was going with the paddle, but, having had four beers, if he went with the paddle too much, he was going to fall facedown in the tub. Paul said as long as it wasn't butt first, not to worry about it.

Occasionally, during the hours we labored, somebody would show up—Caroline, the housekeeper, or Joanne or one of Paul's kids. But they had the good sense to stop at the door. The smell of vintage horse piss and mold had now commingled with the aroma of Budweiser and the salad dressing ingredients, a combination that did not exactly beckon. So they stood near the door and announced that dinner was ready, or Aunt Margaret was here, or the police wanted to invalidate Paul's driver's license, but Paul said we still had work to do, whereupon everyone seemed to scatter in a hurry. No one dared venture into that place. It was forbidding, or sanctified, maybe.

The precise number of giveaway bottles were lined up on the dirt floor like a battalion of infantry soldiers, but there was still a quantity of dressing left in the tub. That's when it occurred to Paul that we could bottle the rest, hustle them into some upscale local food stores, make a buck, and go fishing. But Hotch, a refugee from law school, put on the brakes: "It's against the law," he shouted. "Look at this place! The bugs can't even stay alive here! If somebody croaks from ingesting this stuff, you'll be in court, with no liability insurance. You could wind up without your basement and everything above it. There are certain rules and regulations to be followed—hygienic, first and foremost, proper labeling, government stuff!"

With his barn at stake, Paul agreed that they'd have to take out insurance, create a proper label, and get a bona fide bottler and see if it would sell.

And that is how our baby got started—not in a manger, but in a tub—not a wise man in sight—a fading movie star and a cantankerous writer, but that was it.

You can get straight As in marketing and

still flunk ordinary life.

—NEWMAN TO LEE IACOCCA
AFTER IACOCCA'S PINTO
CAUGHT FIRE

CHAPTER

2

It is 1982, and we are sitting in the conference room of the largest marketing company in America. A long, burnished table is presided over by its president, with five of his department heads in attendance, all experts in how to market new products in the United States. Very imposing. On the table in front of us we have a bottle, once filled with Chianti, now containing an olive oil and vinegar salad dressing, which is the object of this meeting.

"You gentlemen have come to the right place," the president tells us. "We launch new products for some of the biggest brands in America—Libby's, Heinz, Del Monte, Campbell's, Kraft—so we can give you an exponential trajectory on the welter of details that have to be accomplished to launch your salad dressing.

"It's essential to know in advance how the public will react to your product. So we would dispatch people across the country to gather together focus groups of varied ethnicity, financial strata, age groups, sexual preference, fast-food habits, footwear use or nonuse, deodorants, the whole load. We would go around the country, asking folks in shopping malls and such places how they like the bottle, the name, the taste—we'd have them sample it on

lettuce, tomatoes, onions, cabbage, sausage. Then the price—
you have to set a price for us—questions like that, and then in
maybe seven or eight sections of the country we'd correlate the
results and study them to let you know how to adjust all those
things to maximize your introductory impact."

"What would that cost?" we ask.

"Depending on the focus depth, somewhere between three
hundred and four hundred thousand dollars. Now once you're
ready to roll out the product, you'll have to learn how to attend
to distribution, promotion and advertising, public relations—our
experience is with the big guys—Heinz, Kraft, etc., and they figure to spend a million dollars to launch a new product—that's
the general rule the first year. We'll teach you how to muscle into
the big stores—you'll have to make deals, especially with outfits
like A&P and Kroger's—discounts, two-for-ones, free stuff, just
to get your bottle on the shelf—and then how to avoid winding
up on the bottom shelf, down below the packed rows of Krafts
and Wishbones, which have all the eye-level spaces. The odds
on new products are about the same as roulette. Even the biggest
companies have had expensive failures—Campbell's refrigerated
soups, Gerber's 'adult' food line, Nabisco's giant-size Oreo cookies. And then there's the history of celebrity products—which
Karen will tell you about."

"Celebrity products fall into a category of their own," said
Karen, a trim blonde in a tailored suit. "That doesn't refer to fic-
tional characters like Aunt Jemima, Betty Crocker, and Sara
Lee. Nor does it mean endorsers, like the sport stars that appear
on Wheaties boxes. But when celebrities come out with their
own products—Rocky Graziano's spaghetti sauce, Mickey
Mantle's barbecue sauce, Nolan Ryan's All-Star Fruit Snacks,
Gloria Vanderbilt's salad dressing, Reggie Jackson's candy bar,

Carl Yastrzemski's Big Yaz Bread, Diane von Furstenberg's facial tissue, Bill Blass's chocolates, Polly Bergen's Turtle Oil, Marilyn Monroe's Merlot, Fess Parker's wine, James Darren's spaghetti sauce, Phyllis Diller's Philli Dilli Chili, Richard Simmons's Salad Spray, Tommy Lasorda's spaghetti sauce, Yves St. Laurent's cigarettes, Frank Sinatra's neckties—all examples of products these famous people promoted with unsatisfactory results. Take Graziano, for example. He was a popular prizefighter, middleweight champ, big fights with Tony Zale, and as an entertainment personality he appeared in a series of television shows and all kinds of television sitcoms and whatnot. Rocky promoted the hell out of his sauce, but after an initial surge, it simply died and dropped off the shelves—shoppers bought one curiosity jar and that was it. There's never been a real celebrity success in the food business. We estimate the total start-up loss for celebrity products somewhere close to nine hundred million dollars.

"People are serious about their food dollars. They're not at the dinner table to be entertained, they're there to enjoy the food they're eating, which they've purchased within their budgets."

"Now don't be too discouraged by all of this," the president said as Hotch's face dropped in discouragement. "There's always a first time. But no one can predict public response—politics, automobiles, fashion, music, name it. It's a crapshoot, but if we canvass our focus groups and we adjust your product to respond to it, and if you have the capital to get through the losses of the first year, I'd say the odds would be fifty-five to forty-five against flopping."

"No offense, Mr. Newman," Karen said, "but just because they liked you as Butch Cassidy doesn't mean they'll like your salad dressing."

"Maybe we should call it Redford's Own."

"They wouldn't like it any better."

"I'd like to have someone to blame."

We thanked them for their time and said we'd think it over. We said nothing on the walk across the parking lot to Newman's Volkswagen, the rear seat of which had been removed to accommodate a small block Ford V-8.

After we got rolling, we discussed what we had just heard and decided that it would be better to devise a plan of our own: Gather a dozen or so friends and neighbors to a blind tasting that would pit our dressing against all the leading brands, thereby spending $40 rather than $400,000. Then Paul suggested that we each put up $20,000 for starters, causing Hotch to pitch forward and hit his head on the dashboard, the sum of $20,000 making him light-headed, claiming that $20,000 was beyond his grasp. But he admitted he had $12,000 in hand, which he claimed was racetrack winnings that he owed in back rent, despite the fact that he owned his house. So it was decided that we would split the "brainstorming" responsibilities. Hotch would do the legwork and Paul would put up the seed money.

By the time we were on the open road, traveling at Newman's usual 90 mph pace, we both felt pretty good about the afternoon, having saved $1,320,000.

Whenever I do something good, right

away I've got to do something bad so

I know I'm not going to pieces.

—PAUL TO JOANNE AFTER
HE FELL OUT OF THE TREEHOUSE,
BEVERLY HILLS, CALIFORNIA, 1985

CHAPTER

3

Actually, the Newman's Own moniker was originally intended not for a bottle of salad dressing, but for a restaurant that we intended to open in Westport, which is where we both live. The notion of opening a Newman's Own restaurant arose one afternoon while we were out fishing in our boat, the *Caca de Toro*, a rather disreputable craft with a vintage outboard motor, which, on occasion, rebelled in the middle of the Long Island Sound, necessitating an ignominious tow to the marina by a harbor police boat. During our fishing expeditions, we consumed a generous quantity of beer, but, sad to say, we never caught a single noteworthy fish—an occasional sea robin, eel, hermit crab, sand shark, plenty of jellyfish, and plastic containers, but nothing you could put in a frying pan.

Anglers around us would be reeling in bluefish, stripers, flounder, weakfish, and blacks, while we watched with virginal envy, drowning our sorrow in Budweiser. We once went fishing on Man o' War Cay in the Bahamas, noted for its abundance of bonefish and for the expertise of its famous guide, Captain Sam. We spent three days at it, with Captain Sam groaning and grunting at the tiller, after which he announced his retirement.

So since we were not catching lunch on this particular day, our thoughts turned to food. But we couldn't think of a local restaurant that appealed to us.

I think we should open a restaurant, PL said.

Where would it be?

Who knows? Maybe close to the dock so we don't have to walk too far.

You're going to build a brand-new building in that parking lot?

Fella has to be somewhere. I've got a name for it—Newman's Own. It would be a simple American restaurant: great hamburgers—20–21 percent fat, through the grinder twice—fresh corn on the cob, potato skins, a vast salad bar with my salad dressing, knockout desserts, and vintage wines. What a kick to order a $5 hamburger [we're talking 1980], with a $100 bottle of Château Lafitte.

Uh-huh. And how do you see us in this restaurant?

Oh, I'd tend bar and you'd be the Jolly Greeter.

Uh-huh, people are going to come from all over to be at the bar with this famous movie actor, sitting there with their martinis, taking close-ups with their Instamatics, clinking glasses with the superstar, that it?

Pretty picture, isn't it?

Uh-huh. Well, how about this picture? In comes a party of eight oystermen and their wives, all permed and perfumed for the occasion, a couple of rounds of martinis, then the eight oystermen go to the Jolly Greeter and say, "Where is the superstar bartender we have come all the way from Gloucester to clink a glass with?" Oh, says the Jolly Greeter, at the moment he's sunning himself, in between takes, on the beach at Bali-Bali. Sorry. Whereupon the eight oystermen, having come all the way from

Gloucester with their permed and perfumed wives, kick the be-jesus out of the Jolly Greeter.

Well, Hotch, there's a price for everything.

Over the following weeks we scoured the territory for that special place where the Newman's Own eatery could raise its banner—an Italian restaurant, II Villano, had just closed down; there was a Chinese restaurant leaving its premises on the second floor of a building on Carriage Hill; a furniture store in a landmark building on the river was being converted into a hotel with a contemplated restaurant on the top floor—but none grabbed us for our epicurean haven. Our quest somewhat petered out when Newman departed for a film shoot, but he called often from his trailer to discuss the Newman's Own restaurant venture.

One day the two of them ran into a friend of a friend, late of the restaurant business, now in shoes, who flatly stuck his finger in PL's chest and said, "We were always filled to the rafters but no profit. I was skimmed to death, skimmed! Waiters in collusion with the cashier! [This is before computers, remember.] They saved up all the cash register chits in ten-cent increments from $2.50 up into the hundreds. Guy gets a check for $49.50, they go into the chit collection, get a chit for $49.50, guy pays the bill, nothing rung up on the cash register, they pocket the $49.50, and—which really frosted my ass—they get the tip as a bonus!"

The finger was removed from PL's chest and so, apparently, was the idea of opening a restaurant.

CHAPTER

4

After our somewhat dismaying experience with the marketing gurus, we decided to confront our competition by visiting a local supermarket, one of those block-long behemoths that stock every item in the food spectrum, even those in orbit. The initial impact of the salad dressing section was rather overwhelming, to say the least. Section after section, a solid wall of every conceivable kind of dressing, but as we randomly inspected the bottles, it was clear that they all contained chemicals to preserve them, sweeteners in some form or other, artificial coloring, gums, all the things our all-natural Newman's Own was eliminating.

The possibility of putting a dent in this glass barricade, however, was rather daunting, but then again the challenge is what made it interesting. For us, hustling our bottle of salad dressing was a lark, an open-end adventure. We two Davids against those endless shelves of Kraft and Wishbone Goliaths. We'd give it a shot, $40,000 worth, but when it was spent we'd fold our tent, like when you blow your designated wad in Las Vegas and head for the exits. Our odds were about the same as roulette, but what the hell—we'd get a bottler, make a label, take out insurance, and let 'er rip.

From the very beginning, we bucked tradition. When the experts said that something was "always done" in a certain way, we'd do it our way, which was sometimes the very opposite. So instead of a traditional bottle, we had first tried to find a wine bottle, but when we learned that assembly-line machinery couldn't handle a long-necked bottle, or any of the other unusual shapes we preferred, we finally had to settle for a rather traditional container.

Finding someone to bottle the dressing was the most difficult part of getting under way. We heard of a gentleman vintner in upstate Connecticut who had a small vineyard and bottled the white wine he produced. We motored upstate to see his operation, but as it turned out, his assembly line consisted of five high school kids who came in after school. One of them filled the bottles, one by one, from a spigot on the cask, another pounded in the cork, the third stuck on a label, the fourth put a seal on the cork, and the fifth put the bottle in the case box. Needless to say, this after-school crew was not the solution for bottling our salad dressing. We also traveled to a plant in North Carolina to see a major bottler, who, as it turned out, was interested only in runs of one hundred thousand or more.

We considered taking on a partner, and with that in mind we approached the Bigelow Tea Company in neighboring Norwalk. But they were unenthusiastic about the potential for our salad dressing and turned us down. We even toyed with the notion of setting up our own bottling plant in a nearby vacant facility that had once housed a bottler, but the prospect of hiring workers and running such a plant was too daunting.

Hotch made an appointment with a mayonnaise bottler in Brooklyn, and, unfamiliar with the Bushwick section where it was located, he naively drove there in his 1961 Corvette, bright red with white panels; this was an ominous neighborhood where automobiles disappear in a wink. Hotch trepidatiously parked in front of the bottler's plant, fearing that he had seen the last of his 'Vette. But he decided to sacrifice his Corvette to gain a bottler that might result in an annual income that would exceed the pittance on which he lived. There was a kid standing there—said his name was Joey—to whom Hotch gave $2 to keep his eye on the car, for whatever that was worth.

Hotch was frisked and escorted to a crowded office, where, through the thick haze of cigar smoke, he was faced with a group of five men who lounged on chairs arranged around a large central desk. They wore bright neckties and sported diamond rings on their pinkies. Hotch was offered a seat, a cigar, and a glass of Sambuca. Hotch loathed Sambuca, but he downed it bravely. The men were obviously in the middle of a heated discussion, which they tabled temporarily. The guy behind the desk, who had hands the size of catcher's mitts, did the talking.

"So, kid, you're into salad dressing with this Newman actor and you're lookin' to get it bottled, right? Okay. You're usin' olive oil? Good. That's where we come in. In fact, that's where we are. Take a look at that glass case over there. . . . No, not the one with the guns, the one with the Umbria olive oil. That's us—we got olive oil by the balls. You use our olive oil, we bottle your dressing, you'll have dressing by the balls. Show him the line, Sal."

Sal stood up, the size of an NBA center gone to seed, and led Hotch through a door that opened into an area where an assembly line was filling bottles of mayonnaise. Hotch was expecting a scrubbed Hellmann's-esque scene with white-robed, hair-capped workers tending rows of antiseptically serviced jars; instead, he saw a line of disheveled people, wearing a variety of

rather ratty street clothes, no covering on hands or hair, desulto-
rily filling jars as they moved past on a slow-moving belt. Sal was
probably named after Salmonella.

"Well, kid," said the Godfather behind the desk, "we'll spring
for the olive oil and we split fifty-fifty, but we got to go with the
Umbria name, not this—what'd you call it?"

"Newman's Own."

"No, you ain't."

"I'll let you know."

"What's to know? We got a deal."

"I've got to talk to Newman."

"Why?"

"He's my partner."

"Call him up."

"I can't bother him now."

"Why not?"

"His doctor says he's dying."

"Call him up."

"Right! I've got his number in the car. I'll be right back."

There are still track marks from the 'Vette's rubber, bearing
indelible testimony to Hotch's frightened foot on the throttle.

CHAPTER 5

It was Newman's insistent desire to market the dressing that kept Hotch in motion. Scarcely a day passed but what Paul was calling from some unlikely place to discuss a newly discovered source for the perfect olive oil, the perfect red wine vinegar, the perfect mustard, and so on, which he constantly sought. He phoned Hotch from racetracks, in between his races, from mobile dressing rooms on location while shooting *Absence of Malice* and *The Verdict*, from airports on his way to make speeches on behalf of the nuclear freeze movement, and even, on one occasion, from where he was making a coffee commercial for a Japanese film crew, a background of cacophonous Nipponese chatter making it difficult to hear him.

The overriding purpose of these phone calls was to get his dressing into a bottle, a bottle bearing the Newman's Own name on a proper label, a bottle ready for public display, a bottle that would allow us to thumb our noses at the naysayers.

Paul had always been perverse about complacency. It was his theory that he had to keep things off balance or it's finito. That's why he took up racing cars when they said, Not when you're forty-seven years old, you out of your mind? It took him ten years to learn the ropes, but doggedness got him there, an old guy winning four national titles. That perversity also accounted for many of his risky movie roles, going where he hadn't been before, running the risk of falling on his face. Running the same risk with the salad dressing. A movie guy and his writer buddy going hard against the odds. Like Butch and Sundance jumping off a cliff into a business and marketing canyon—the fall will get us if the sharks in the supermarkets don't. It was a lunatic thing, like a bumblebee or a helicopter. There's no reason for it to fly, but then again, there were the Wright brothers.

When Paul was in college, he had demonstrated a knack for getting a business invention to fly. He was attending Kenyon College in Gambier, Ohio, when, to augment his dwindling GI Bill funds, he went into the laundry business.

The school's laundry company used to visit the dorms, going from room to room to pick up individual laundry; then Paul made a deal with the company for a much lower rate to pick up the laundry at one site in the town. Paul rented an abandoned storefront in a partially developed part of Gambier, on a dirt road of sorts there, fixed it up, and advertised in the school paper that his laundry service would serve free beer to any customer bringing in his laundry. Figuring the cost of a keg of beer, plus rent and the laundry's charges, against what he charged for the laundry, Paul was able to turn a profit of $80 a week, which by today's conversion amounts to about $500. Paul finally sold the business in his senior year to a friend of his, but as luck would have it, a month or so later one of the customers who had overimbibed the free beer put on a boxing glove, staggered out into the street, and started to masturbate a horse that was tied up there. The authorities shut down the business, busting the whole shop.

We kept looking for a bottler, running down this lead and that, but those fruitless experiences began to dampen our enthusiasm. There came a day, however, when we were ordering corned beef sandwiches at a local delicatessen, that it occurred to us to ask the owner if he knew of any local bottler. "No," he said, pausing midslice, "but I have a customer who is a food broker—maybe he could help you."

The broker was a short, compact, natty man named David Kalman, who exuded a veteran salesman's frothy optimism. Affiliated with a small outfit, Northeast Brokerage, David had been hustling food products all his life. We met with him and explained our need for a small-time bottler, just a few bottles, which he said was no problem (his favorite words), but a short time later, it became obvious that there was a problem because he appeared with two men who submitted a written proposal whereby the three of them would form a company to produce the dressing and pay Newman a royalty. One of the men was an investment banker, and the other was a former Nabisco executive. Obviously, we had gotten off to a false start—no partners, David, no entrepreneurs with promises, a *bottler*, David, someone with a small bottling plant, get it? David got it. "Okay," he said, "I misunderstood."

The fact that David Kalman's group had shown such interest served to reinforce our attempt to get started. We got in touch with a friend of ours who had been chief executive at General Electric (Jack Welsh had worked for him) and a top banana at both RJR Nabisco and Standard Brands. We asked him what he thought of our chances with our dressing in the marketplace. "Well," he said, "you're up against Kraft, which has fifteen facings, and you're up against Wishbone and half a dozen other name brands, so I don't think you have a prayer. You'd be better off selling it by mail order. Put a little ad in the back of *The New Yorker*, for example, announcing Paul Newman is making his own salad dressing—people will send you their checks and you can send them a bottle by mail."

We were getting a lot of advice from those so-called experts in the field, all of whom were either trying to convince us to avoid the certified disaster that we were headed for or offering squirrelly solutions like selling the dressing by mail order. None of the big commercial bottlers took us seriously. After we rejected several of David's improvisations, his enthusiasm began to wane, but he finally did locate a bottler named Andy Crowley, who was exactly the kind of bottler we were seeking; Crowley ran Ken's, a small bottling plant outside Boston that made bottled dressing for Ken's Steakhouse, a modest Boston restaurant, and a private-label dressing for Stop & Shop, where Crowley's father was a salad dressing buyer.

Kalman arranged to meet with Crowley at Boston's Logan Airport, but first he needed the formula for the dressing at this time. Paul was packing to go someplace, but before taking off, he paused to scribble the ingredients for the dressing on a brown paper bag, which is what Kalman showed Crowley at the airport meeting.

Andy Crowley recalls: "David Kalman called me and said he represented the Newhotch Company—I guess that's what they called it before Newman's Own—and requested that I meet him at Logan Airport to hear a proposition that he had on behalf of this new company. I had never met Kalman, but he had a reputation for being shrewd and aggressive, so I decided to check him out. He explained that his clients were the movie star Paul Newman and the author who wrote Hemingway's biography among other things, and he explained about this dressing that

Paul wanted to bottle and sell in the stores. He showed me a formula scrawled on the back of a paper bag. I decided to look into it, but on going back to my office, I sent a memo to my then partner, which I still have: 'These people might prove to be a bunch of flakes—an actor and an author, and worst of all, a salesman, but it will cost us very little to see how serious they are.'

"I gave the formula to our production department and asked them to turn out a sample as quickly as they could. What was unusual about it was that unlike the other dressings that had the majority of bottles on the supermarket shelves, dressings made with low oil content, white cider vinegar, dehydrated onion, and garlic, all of which saves a lot of money, this formula that David handed me used none of the tools of preservation."

Andy later explained to us that since the formula on the paper bag did not contain gums and chemical chelating agents, it would spoil in a short time; he urged us to add some of the chemicals that would fix its longevity. We refused. Our dressing was to be touted as "all-natural," and that meant no chemicals whatsoever.

Reluctantly, Andy agreed to submit our formula to his chemist. "All-natural" was a term that was unheard of in connection with dressings, so he had little hope for its prospects.

But to Andy's surprise, after testing, his chemists concluded that since Paul's dressing consisted of oil and vinegar and contained mustard, those elements combined to form a natural gum. We were elated with this lucky happenstance, but Andy presented us with another problem. We did not have EDTA (ethylenediaminetetraaceticacid) in our formula, which was thought to be essential in preserving life span on the shelf. "If a bottled dressing cannot stay on the shelf for somewhere in the neighborhood of a year," Andy explained, "it will not be acceptable to the supermarkets. EDTA is the only means available to bind the iron and copper that occur in water, and, if not bound, the iron and copper will have a disastrous effect on the oil.

"You fellows got lucky on the gum, but now you're trying to reinvent the wheel. All those big outfits have chemists who've been using these fixes for as long as I've been in business. The food business is a very practical affair—whatever you put in a bottle has to have shelf life or forget it. Let's try half of the usual EDTA. What about it?"

We didn't budge. All-natural meant positively no chemicals.

Andy's chemists gave him a hard time about it, but eventually they put our formula through the longevity test. The result was not what they expected. They found that in the process of making mustard, in grinding the whole mustard seed, a layer of mucus is released that is a natural gum and did everything that EDTA did, but did it naturally. Another unexpected factor that worked in our favor: The olive oil (no other dressing used olive oil at that time because it was too expensive) is so nutty and has so much flavor that even if there was a touch of rancidity, it would not be noticeable, whereas soybean oil, which was the oil commonly used at that time, would smell and taste of the rancidity much more quickly.

"My own take on Paul's salad dressing," Andy says, "was that it was certainly different from anything that was in a bottle at that time. The ingredients that were called for—the red wine vinegar, olive oil, mustard—made it more expensive, but also gave it a more particular flavor, a richer flavor. Red wine, which to my knowledge had not been used in any other dressings, gave it a totally different taste, and my personal preference was against the very strong flavors of Wishbone and Kraft. I particularly didn't like that they were salty as hell.

"Now we had the problem of getting the proper balance of the ingredients. Over the succeeding weeks, I went back and forth, trying to produce a bottled dressing that Newman and Hotchner would approve, but every time we sent a sample, they came back with new requests and we'd have to put in this, that, and the other thing. We finally backed away from the whole thing. In the beginning, I'd had my qualms about dealing with an actor and a writer, and it looked like my initial assessment was correct. The requests were simply too much for us to handle. Why can't we use whole ground peppercorns rather than just ground pepper? And can you put it in a wine bottle rather than a regular bottle? Why can't we use fresh garlic and onion instead of dehydrated? And can you put a twig in it, like a twig of thyme? We were slowly going nuts."

In the beginning, Andy had not only had serious misgivings about the formula Paul had scribbled on the paper bag and the way we were fussing about the taste, he was also skeptical about the seriousness of this risky bottling venture with a movie star's name on it but not a company behind it. Risky, also, because no one had bottled an all-natural, no-preservatives dressing before with a preponderance of olive oil, a different kind of vinegar, and herbs and spices untried in bottled dressing. In addition, Andy knew that even if he could produce a viable dressing from this paper bag formula, there was little chance that a bottle of it could squeeze its way onto supermarket shelves that were already overstocked with a dozen different Kraft dressings, another dozen Wishbones, plus Hidden Valley, Marzetti's, Henry and Henry, Bernstein's, and countless others.

It was one thing for us to mix up a batch in Paul's kitchen, but quite another thing to produce the same result in a commercial bottling plant. Over a period of six months, Andy sent us thirty or more samples, but each time we asked for additional tweaking, trying to get ingredients balanced exactly the way we wanted them, so that the unique zesty taste of the dressing when we mixed it in Paul's kitchen would be duplicated in the bottle. It didn't help that Paul was in front of the camera somewhere or other or that Hotch was busy with some theater or literary pursuit.

When Andy informed us that he was giving up on us, it meant we had to start all over again, disheartened but still determined to make it work.

Just when things look darkest,

they go black.

—P. L. NEWMAN TO
WALTER MONDALE, 1948

CHAPTER

6

We decided that before we went through the arduous process of searching for a new bottler, we should find out how we stacked up against the competition. Were the Krafts and Wishbones equal to or better tasting than ours? If so, we should perhaps abandon our effort, which already looked pretty futile. So we organized a competitive tasting in the kitchen of a local caterer we knew named Martha Stewart, who, along with her husband, Andrew, occasionally catered dinner parties at our homes. We filled twenty matching bowls with samples of the popular brands, one of those bowls with our dressing, put numbers on the bowls but no other identification, and invited twenty or so friends and neighbors to sample the lot of them. We had glasses of water for palate cleansing and a mountain of lettuce leaves to dip in the dressing. The tasters had pads on which to evaluate each dressing on a scale of one to ten. The fate of our dressing now hung in the balance. If we scored poorly, we'd probably give up the ghost.

Our guinea pig tasters took their time, dipping, chewing, cleansing, tabulating, and the wait for us was pretty excruciating, like waiting for reviews on opening night. All but two ballots had us number one, and on those two we were ranked second. Martha also thought that we beat out the competition, but she suggested that the flavor of our dressing would be improved if we added a fresh bay leaf to each bottle. Kalman said that that probably would improve the taste, but since the bottles would be on a conveyor belt being filled at sixty a minute, it would be rather impossible to put workers on the assembly line who could move fast enough to drop a bay leaf in the bottles as they scurried by. The marketing corporation we had first consulted would probably have scoffed at the meagerness of our sampling, but for us, this verdict proved that we were on the right track. It was then and there that Paul anointed us Salad King (referring to himself as the Salad King of New England), and the following day, his lawyer, Leo Nevas, incorporated us using his office as the corporation's address. As yet we didn't have a label or insurance—as a matter of fact, we didn't even have a bottled product—but we now had a couple of titles: P. L. Newman, president, and A. E. Hotchner, vice president, of Salad King, Inc.

CHAPTER

7

While we were once again investigating possible bottlers, we were also trying to devise a label for the bottle-to-be. We had been warned by food gurus that it was very tricky business to produce an acceptable food label. They advised us to use only those few graphic artists who specialized in designing labels. Of course, all we had to hear was how things were *always* done for us not to do it that way. Paul had a racing buddy, Sam Posey, whose wife, Ellen, was an artist, whom he contacted. Although she had never done graphics before, she was willing to take a stab at it. Our first idea was to have a label that looked like parchment, but those early attempts proved to be too bland to stand up against competitive labels.

At this time Paul was driving for an old friend of his, Bob Sharp, who owned the factory-sponsored Datsun (now Nissan) race team, and it was on the way to a race at Lime Rock that Paul mentioned our salad dressing adventure. Bob suggested that we meet with his friend Stew Leonard, who owned a big supermarket in neighboring Norwalk.

We subsequently had lunch with Stew, who warned us (as we had heard many times by now) that his attempts to sell celebrity products had fizzled—Roger Staubach's peanut butter, Graziano's spaghetti sauce (which he said wouldn't sell even in Pittsburgh)—and he said that those products didn't sell because the products themselves were nothing special. "If your dressing is really good," Stew said, "you've got a good shot at it since you'll sell the first bottle because your face is on the label."

"Whoa!" Paul said. "My face is on the label?"

"Of course. How else do you get their attention? You said you weren't going to advertise, so how will the customer know it's you?"

"It'll say Newman's Own."

"For all they know, that could be Seymour Newman from Newark, New Jersey. You will not be able to sell bottle one unless your face is on the label, that's for sure."

"My face on a bottle of salad dressing? Not a chance in hell."

"Not if the stuff is good. You'll be doing the customers a big favor. Tell you what . . . I'd like to set up a tasting. If your dressing is something special and you have a good label on it, I'll get Andy Crowley at Ken's to bottle it and I'll kick off your sales with a big promotion at my store."

"We don't think you'll get anywhere with Crowley. He already turned us down."

"Gentlemen," Stew said, "I am Andy's best customer—I sell more Ken's than all his other customers combined. If your dressing measures up, I assure you he will bottle it."

☞ We are on the *Caca de Toro*, mock fishing. The president and vice president of Salad King are having an executive meeting, not knowing which will sink first—the boat or the business. Paul is still brooding over the tacky suggestion that he put his face on a bottle of salad dressing. Even though we weren't flushed with expectation, if it was necessary to do that in order to float the venture, it would be a new low in exploitation. Paul felt, "Put my face on the windshield of a Mercedes-Benz or a Volvo, maybe . . . but salad dressing?"

We floated along for a while, glumly watching the non-bobbing bobbers. Hotch suggested that perhaps the time had come to bag the whole idea. The bobber dipped and Paul reeled in a hermit crab.

"You know, there could be a kind of justice here, Hotch. I go on television all the time to hustle my films. TV gets me and my time for free, and the film gets exposure for free—mutual and circular exploitation, so to speak. Now then, if we were to go the lowest of the low road and plaster my face on a bottle of oil and vinegar dressing just to line our pockets, it would stink. But to go the low road to get to the high road—shameless exploitation for charity, for the common good—now there's an idea worth the hustle, a reciprocal trade agreement."

Then he and the hermit crab went in for a swim.

If we ever have a plan,

we're screwed!

—PN TO HIMSELF
AT A STORK CLUB URINAL

CHAPTER

8

Stew Leonard called Andy Crowley and said that he had received a call from Paul Newman, who had come to see him at his store. "He asked me whether I could bottle his salad dressing in my milk plant, on the same line where I bottle milk, but I explained to him that there's no compatibility. I brought him over to the section that we have with your Ken's dressings, and suggested that you do the bottling for him. But Paul said, 'Well, I've already been dealing with Crowley, but he gave up.'"

Andy admitted that was true, because "they were asking for whole peppercorns, cloth labels, 'Can I put a twig in?' . . . Nuts! These guys don't know what they're doing."

Stew agreed but asked Andy to come down to his store to discuss the situation. "We have had a big tasting here in the store, and Newman's dressing rated at the top, so we should figure out a way to do this."

At the meeting, Stew acted as referee and facilitator. Paul had brought a bottle of his dressing and a bag full of lettuce leaves, and all through the meeting he kept dipping lettuce in the dressing and munching it. Andy spent two hours explaining the fundamentals of the business, and at one point, Andy recalls, "when

I mentioned a cash discount, Paul interrupted me and asked, 'What's that?'"

Finally, after hours of discussion, Stew interjected himself and said, "Okay, Andy, enough! I want to go ahead on this. I'll buy two thousand cases. Are you going to make it?"

"What was I going to say," Andy says, "other than okay, because he was one of my biggest customers, and if I had said no, I would have been out of that store in a hurry—he would have filled up my car with whatever was left of Ken's dressing on the shelf and I would be on my way back to Boston.

"But before I left, I extracted a concession from Paul and Hotch. I pointed out that I had eliminated the gums and the EDTA, but that fresh garlic and onion were adding elements that would very likely curdle the entire mix. No one has ever used them fresh because they would be active and volatile. I put my foot down—they would have to use dehydrated like everyone else. It's all-natural, it's just dehydrated. Okay?"

We reluctantly acquiesced, our first concession to tradition, but it was a decision we would soon regret.

And he asked himself,

Good Lord, what have we unleashed?

—THE SALAD KING TO
A. E. HOTCHNER, HONG KONG, 1982

CHAPTER

9

We are now in business, but we are determined that it not turn into *serious* business. We devise a mock Napoleonic "N" with a laurel wreath around it for the neck of the bottle. On the label we poke fun at the usual corny hype on our competitors' bottles with *Nomen Vide Optima Expecta* ("See the Name, Expect the Best"), *Tutto Naturale*, and in place of a copyright notice, we have "Appellation Newman Contrôlée." As a spoof of businesses that tout their ancestry, our slogan is "Fine Foods Since February." On the rear panel of the bottle, we composed the first of the many legends that will eventually appear on all our products.

> Why? Why market this all-natural, no-nonsense, kick-in-the-derrière dressing? In a word—the neighbors. For years, at Christmas, old pal Hotchner and I bottled this concoction for friends. The acclaim was deafening, the repeat orders staggering. This year, they chained us to the furnace until we brewed 30 gallons—a prisoner of

my own excellence. Enough, I said! Let's go public!
I'm out of the basement and onto the shelf!

—P. Loquesto Newman

After a dozen or so excellent versions, Ellen Posey produced a label acceptable to our president, we have signed off on Andy Crowley's formula for our dressing, we now have appropriate insurance, and Ken's slow-moving assembly line is turning out our first batch of bottles. Stew Leonard has posted a prominent announcement on the huge signboard located adjacent to the Post Road outside his supermarket: WELCOME, PAUL NEWMAN. This was a big mistake, because hundreds of shoppers packed the store, refused to leave, and gridlocked the premises. As a sales gimmick, Stew had positioned a mound of lettuce next to the rows of Newman's Own bottles with a large sign above them: PAUL NEWMAN'S SALAD DRESSING, $1.19. BUY TWO JARS, ONE HEAD OF LETTUCE FREE. Shameless exploitation was alive and well. Next to the sign was an enormous photograph of the two of us in Butch Cassidy costumes with Stew between us; a large sign above the photograph proclaimed: BUTCH CASSIDY IS ALSO A GOURMET COOK. In two weeks' time, ten thousand bottles were sold and Ken's had to put on extra shifts for their production line.

We looked upon the Stew Leonard sales as a local phenomenon, however, so we still planned to confine our distribution to local stores; but then we began to receive inquiries about the product from the likes of A&P and Grand Union. David Kalman reported that he received a call from a specialty food importer, one of the biggest in the Midwest, who ordered a truckload.

Paul told David to turn them down. "Explain that we're just a little local outfit that will only sell locally." David's salesman's instinct rebelled—turn down A&P? All the big supermarkets? David had a vision of winged commissions flying out the window. "You can't," he said adamantly. "It's against the law. There's a federal statute against discriminating sales." David was referring to the Robinson-Patman Act, which makes it "unlawful for any person to discriminate in favor of one purchaser against another purchaser or purchasers of a commodity . . ." Faced with this reality, we knew that Newman's Own would now have to bust its restraints and have a life of its own. Our little joke, our whimsical $40,000 adventure, was like a character in a play or characters being developed in a book who suddenly take off and run away from the writer, and all you can do is say, Look at that little bugger go. We didn't know where Newman's Own was taking us, but it definitely had a head of steam.

☛ We didn't have an office, a bookkeeper, or any other employees, not even a telephone. For starters, our lawyer's bookkeeper helped set up our books, and we rented a two-room office across the hall from his office, which was located above a bank on the Post Road in Westport. Because we were operating on the original $40,000 investment ($20,000 remained after paying for labels and so forth), we felt we were on shaky ground. So instead of buying office furniture, Paul decided that since it was September and he was closing his swimming pool, he would simply furnish the office with his pool furniture, even to the extent of keeping a beach umbrella over our shared desk (his picnic table). Paul's Ping-Pong table became our conference table, but the only conferences we held were when we played Ping-Pong. Paul wrote our scores on the low ceiling, but when his losses mounted significantly, he had the ceiling painted. On the wall above our desk we put up a graph that would chart our sales from September, when we first started, to January, beginning from zero.

We were now officially incorporated as an S corporation with Paul as the sole stockholder, which meant a lot of things but mostly that whatever the profits, the company would have to be without any capital every December 31, all profits and royalties paid out, and money would have to be borrowed from a bank starting every January 1 in order to stay in business.

☞ The tradition in the food industry was for the supermarket to pay the broker for the goods shipped; the broker then would take its commission (Advantage Foods took 7 percent) and send the balance to the company. We took one look at this "tradition" and decided that Newman's Own would set a precedent: The supermarkets would pay us directly, and we would pay the broker, thereby getting our money much sooner. We did something else that had never been done before—we arranged with Ken's to pay them in twenty days but required the supermarkets to pay us in *ten*, which meant that we'd always have money on hand to pay for a product that had been shipped. Also, we didn't pay for an inventory. Ken's made shipments only when an order was received, and the bottles were sent from the manufacturer directly to the customer.

We hit upon this arrangement because in our professional

lives we were irritatingly aware that a publisher and a movie company would tie up money due us, based on industry custom, for nine, ten months. The system we devised worked beautifully—in fact, the $20,000 was never spent, and the other $20,000 was recouped six weeks after we went into business.

There are three rules for running

a business; fortunately, we don't

know any of them.

—A. E. HOTCHNER TO
MONICA LEWINSKY AT THE
1998 MISS AMERICA PAGEANT

CHAPTER

10

It was September 1982, and we decided that there had been enough foreplay—it was time to get into the actual act. With our meager capital, we could not afford to advertise, so we decided to make our worldly launch a really tacky but attention-getting event. In keeping with our renegade philosophy, we rejected such glitzy New York City venues as The Four Seasons and "21" in favor of Hanratty's, a grungy bar and grill located at East 90th Street and Second Avenue, an inaccessible, unfashionable area. Kalman invited the head buyers for the big supermarkets, and a freelance publicist we hired sent invitations to the newspapers, television stations, wire services, magazines, the entire media kit and kaboodle. We asked Gene Shalit, who had often interviewed Paul about his movies on the *Today* show, to join in the occasion. To highlight our dressing, Hanratty's would prepare a variety of salads, all using Newman's Own, and there would be an open bar with music provided by a three-piece group of dubious musicality.

We were having lunch at Mario's Place in Westport, discussing the upcoming Hanratty's event and trying to dream up some diverting commotion. Hotch had written salad dressing lyrics to a Gilbert & Sullivan song to be sung at the launch, but we needed someone to sing it.

Paul thought it should be someone unexpected—for instance, Luciano Pavarotti. Hotch agreed that that would be unexpected and certainly get attention but doubted that Pavarotti would be inclined to sing a salad dressing aria. Paul, on the old theory of nothing ventured, nothing gained, made a few calls and found out that Pavarotti could be reached at a hotel in San Francisco. It being nine A.M. on the West Coast, Pavarotti was awakened by the phone call.

Pavarotti had some difficulty unraveling who was calling and why, but when he had it sorted out, he was "*dispiace*" not to be able to oblige but was engaged to sing *Pagliacci* on that date with the San Francisco Opera. At this point, Hotch suggested that with so little time before the event, Paul should sing it himself. "I have a voice like an ice pick," said PL.

"Good," said Hotch, "keep 'em awake."

With three of his lawyer's office help as his backup chorus, this was what Paul sang in his semibaritone debut while the television cameras were rolling:

(To the tune of "I Am the Very Model of a Model Major-General")

I've tasted all the dressings on the shelves at food emporiums,
And most of them taste like they should be served in
　vomitoriums.
I'm very well acquainted too with dressings that you mix at
　home,
And thrust upon the visiting and unsuspecting gastronome.
But as for me I much prefer to eat my salad in the sack,
And that is why in Newman's Own you'll find an aphrodisiac.

CHORUS:

And that is why in Newman's Own
You'll find an aphrodisiac,
And that is why in Newman's Own
You'll find an aphrodisiac,
And that is why in Newman's Own
You'll find an aphrodisi-disi-ac.

Which brings me to the subject of this bottle's true ingredients,
That I will now reveal to you with candor and expedience.
In short, when you have tasted it
You'll know just what you're get-ett-ing,
Feel free to strip and lurch about with naughty pirouet-ett-ing.

CHORUS:

In short, when you have tasted it
You'll know just what you're get-ett-ing,
Feel free to strip and lurch about with naughty pirouet-ett-ing.

To find the proper olive oil we searched through several
*   continents,*
To find the one that had the most extraordinary redolence,
From sunny Spain to Portugal and then on to Transylvania,
How the hell was I to know we'd find the stuff in
*   Pennsylvania?*

And now we had to turn our search a red wine vinegar to find,
And sampling here and sampling there we drunk us got and
*   pretty blind,*
The mustard search was just as far until we learned our lesson,
And found exactly what we sought at Hotchner's delicatessen.

CHORUS:
And found exactly what we sought at Hotchner's delicatessen,
And found exactly what we sought at Hotchner's delicatessen,
And found exactly what we sought at Hotchner's
delica-delica-tess-en.

The clever spices we have added are a well-kept mystery,
And everything is natural to ward off flue and dysent'ry!
So now I have explained to you with all my cogent reasonings,
Why I hope that I am known as the man for all good seasonings!

CHORUS:
So now he has explained to you with all his cogent reasonings,
Why he hopes that he is known as the man for all good
seasonings!

So that Paul would be aided and abetted in this dubious entertainment, Hotch doubled his chutzpah and asked Joanne to sing a salad dressing love song to the tune of Rodgers & Hart's "Where or When."

You're having press people?

TV cameras, the works.

And I croon a love song to a salad dressing?

It's a great Rodgers & Hart melody.

I know the song.

Well, there you are.

But with the original lyrics.

I didn't want Paul to be all alone up there.

Up where?

We built a little stage.

Where?

Hanratty's Bar and Grill.

And you two are really trying to make a go of that salad dressing?

☞ She winced when she saw the lyrics but nevertheless bravely sang:

Some couples frolic in the nude,
Doing things rather lewd.
But for us,
Our aptitude
Was sharing sexy food.
The mem'ry of the meals we ate,
Still makes me salivate,
Tasting things
From off your fork—
Onion rings
On poached pork—
Listen how my stomach sings!

CHORUS:
It seems we sat and ate like this before,
The chopped chicken liver in the pastry shell,
I remember that the smell was swell.
The lox we're eating is the lox we ate,
The bagels and cream cheese really sealed our fate,
You were a virgin and I was celibate.
But when the salad course came to you,
Then you jumped up and said, "We're through!"
But now, my darling, we have Newman's Own

To sprinkle on the salad of our love
Forever more.

The turnout at Hanratty's filled the joint to overflowing: three camera crews, reporters from all the New York newspapers and from the Associated Press, movie people, food critics, and the CEOs of many of the supermarket chains. Paul kept a very steady Gilbert & Sullivan beat, Joanne gave a sexy lilt to her salad dressing love song, and Gene Shalit delivered this monologue:

> Over the years, I have been prepared for great things from Paul Newman, but a prepared salad dressing was not among them. I was naturally on my guard. Caution was called for, so I went back and checked out my reviews of his movies. *Butch Cassidy* was good, and so was *The Sting* . . . but I really felt safe when I noticed that I was one of the few people in America who admired *Quintet*. In fact, I was one of the few people in America who *saw* *Quintet*. So I figured it was safe to *try* a spoonful. I discovered that its unusual flavor comes from a most unusual oil—Mobil One. The mixture was blended with exotic spices in his Datsun crank case. In fact, to test it, Paul first used it in his Datsun 280ZX, which is how he won at Brainard, Minnesota, this year.
>
> They needed a name. A marketing expert was called in—a woman, it so happened—and she suggested "Paul Newman's Undressing." Joanne dismissed her. When Sophia Loren rang me up the other day, I told her that "Paul Newman is putting out a salad dressing." Sophia said, "What came after 'Paul Newman is putting out'?"

A cynic told me that to get to the truth of this project, you need only look at the names of some of Paul's movies: *The Hustler*, *Pocket Money*, and *The Outrage*. I countered with: *Sometimes a Great Notion*.

This is going to be a very special year for Paul: the appearance of Newman's Own here in September . . . and the release in December of *The Verdict*, an exceptional film in which he gives an extraordinary performance. Clearly, these are Paul Newman's salad days.

The Hanratty's event received wide coverage in the United States and abroad, and the following day orders began inundating Kalman, who had now become affiliated with a new brokerage house, Advantage Food Marketing. There were orders from Shopwell, A&P, Stop & Shop, and other chains, and truckload sales were dispersed to buyers all over the country. The usual order for a supermarket was one case a month, but the Newman's Own dressing began to sell at three cases a week. Our whimsical lark had metamorphosed into a real, honest-to-God business, and it caught us off guard.

We quickly expanded to a three-room office with telephones, stationery, a fax machine, and a photocopier. We also acquired a staff or, at least, the beginning of one. Ursula Gwynne, in charge of daily operations (as she would be for the next dozen years), Joan Williams, for bookkeeping (she would eventually become a vice president and treasurer), and Pam Papay, in charge of charity requests. They would soon be joined by Roberta Pearson, Nancy Goodfellow, Marianne Sheldon, and Mitchyco Campbell—those ladies would constitute our entire staff for the first fifteen years of our existence.

It is useless to put on the brakes

when you are upside down.

—O. J. SIMPSON TO HIS LAWYER
IN THE WHITE BLAZER

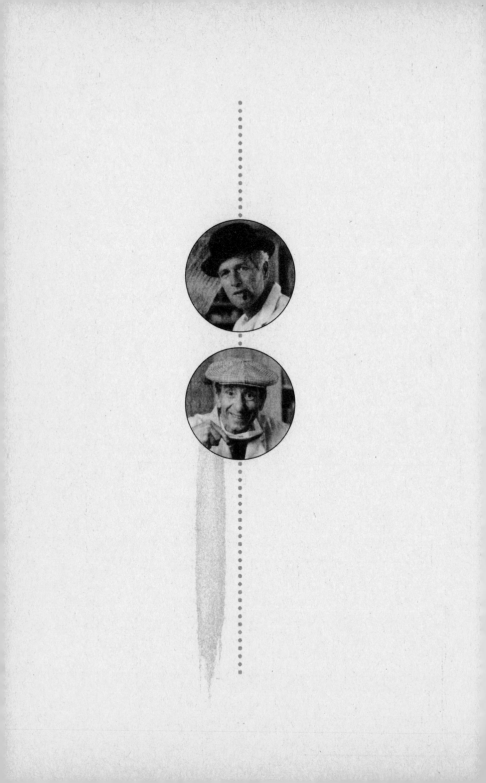

CHAPTER

11

Soon after our debut bottles appeared in the supermarkets, we were jolted by our first critical evaluation, which cropped up in an interview with Paul conducted by Mimi Sheraton, food critic of the *New York Times*:

SEPTEMBER 15, 1982
NEWMAN'S SALAD DRESSING:
OIL, VINEGAR AND BALLYHOO
BY MIMI SHERATON

"The reason I went into the salad-dressing business," Paul Newman said, "is because I suddenly realized I needed a different power base. When Reagan became President, I discovered I had been end-played and that the power base I formerly operated from no longer existed. I realized that to be effective I would have to enter the world of business, and this is it." He explained that the dressing—which actually contains 51 percent olive oil mixed with soybean oil, red wine vinegar, water, lemon juice, spices, salt and dehydrated onion and garlic—is not quite what he would prepare for himself at home.

"This product must have shelf life, which is why we used dehydrated onion and garlic. And if it were all olive oil, it would have to sell for something like $4 or $9 for an eight-ounce bottle, instead of $1.19. Anyone who sells it for much more than that will be profiteering."

Although he listened intently to criticism about the unpleasant oily feel of the dressing and its overpowering dehydrated onion and garlic flavors, Mr. Newman regards his new culinary project with more than a pinch of humor. He said he thought it would be fun to have some French on the label, hence "Appellation Newman Contrôlée" and "L'étoile du vinaigre et de l'huile—l'huile et le vinaigre des étoiles" ("The star of oil and vinegar—the oil and vinegar of the stars").

Mr. Newman said he likes simple American foods such as cucumber sandwiches ("though I wouldn't like to dwell on them"), scrod, haddock, hamburgers, turkey and iceberg lettuce.

Mr. Newman went on: "Some people have sexual dreams, but I dream about food. Then when I wake up I want to eat the food I dreamed about. That means I have to keep a big pantry, because you never know.

"This morning I didn't eat anything," he said, "because I dreamed about liver last night, and I hate liver. This salad dressing is literally something I dreamed up," he continued. "The main part of it in a long night's sleep, and then the adjustments that came in short afternoon naps. It took about a year to come together and was so popular with my family that whenever I had to go away, my five kids made me mix up a huge batch of dressing so they would have it on salads while I was gone.

"I guess I've had more fun doing this than anything else I've done in a long time. But remember, it's really my way of telling Ronald Reagan that his salad days are over."

☛ We were shook up by Mimi's harsh judgment that the dressing suffered from an unpleasant oily feel and overpowering dehydrated onion and garlic flavors. Rather like the principal telling you your child has a learning disorder. Now, despite the dire warnings from Andy Crowley's chemists, we insisted that they try the fresh stuff in sample bottles. We had compromised our standards, but we would never do it again.

Paul called the Ken's chemist directly and told him we absolutely had to find a way to use fresh onion and garlic. The chemist objected, but Paul was adamant. As a result, Ken's experimented with various ways of eliminating the negative effect of fresh onion and garlic, and after much experimentation they found that if the fresh onion and garlic were cut up and combined with the vinegar that was going to be used in the dressing, and if that concoction was marinated for a period of two weeks and then drawn out of the barrel just as it was being added to the dressing, it retained its fresh flavor and eliminated the dehydrated's metallic taste. This enabled us to be the first dressing to use the word *fresh* on the label.

Once that new dressing succeeded in the stores, Kraft and the other big companies quickly switched to fresh onion and garlic, although today dehydrated is again being used in most dressings because it is much easier and cheaper. Nevertheless, Newman's Own still sticks to fresh onion and garlic, even though it has to be bucketed out of a drum by hand, making it very messy to handle. That's the price we were willing to pay in order to get authentic taste. Also, most dressings today are still using apple cider vinegar, which is much cheaper than the red wine vinegar that is used in Newman's Own.

The result was but another instance of our luck in bucking tradition. Not only had our insistence produced a way to use fresh garlic and onion without affecting the dressing's shelf life, but the combination of olive oil, mustard, vinegar, and the other condiments fixed the contents in such a way that the bottle did not require refrigeration after opening. It was rather like Sir Alexander Fleming accidentally discovering the mold that would become penicillin.

☛ Now that the dressing was being produced in such quantity, we were concerned that the quality of the original be maintained (there was the classic case of the mouse in the bottle of Coca-Cola), so we began regularly to drop into supermarkets, pick out one of our bottles at random, take it home, and sample the contents. After a while, we realized that this was not a very scientific method, so we employed a firm, Shuster Inc., that specialized in inspecting factories and in randomly analyzing food products on market shelves. They have sampled our products from coast to coast and abroad for twenty years now, and their meticulous reports enable us to monitor whether our suppliers are adhering to our standards.

"Blue-cheese, Thousand Island, or Paul Newman?"

PART TWO

In Pursuit

CHAPTER
12

Although we had to give our fledgling business serious attention, we were also getting a real kick out of it. We decorated the walls of our cramped offices with epigrams that took corporate pronouncements to a new but not higher level. With the collaboration of our good friend the late Steve Colhoun, a very gifted photographer, we did a series of zany photographs illustrating how we started the business. The day we spent in Paul's barn, Paul as Butch Cassidy, Hotch as a skewed version of Sundance, was rollicking good fun, especially that conjured moment when, with test tube and mixing bowl, the dressing spun to life.

We were also enjoying the phenomenon of customers writing us personal, rather intimate letters, which were certainly not the usual run of customer communication. The brokers said that in their experience, letters written by customers were almost always complaints, but not ours. Our customers wrote to us like members of an extended family. Praises and advice. Letters by the hundreds. In addition to letters of praise, there were letters of gratitude and other such things:

Dear Sirs:

A miracle happened while eating a salad with your delicious dressing. Some dropped on my shoe. I ran and got a paper towel and rubbed it off—haven't seen a shine on my shoes like that for 81 years. Now I use it every day for shining my shoes, and putting it on my salad. Even tried it on furniture and it worked. So, you have a product to double your money. Your sales would go up ten percent if you let people know your dressing is good for shoes and furniture polish.

With your knowledge of products, I am sure you could make a cake out of it for shoe shining.

> J.F.
> Tucson, AZ

Dear People:

Love your Olive Oil and Vinegar Dressing. Perfect on deli sandwiches in adult motels on lazy weekday afternoons. The problem is the bottle.

There I was, astride my boyfriend, king-size bed beneath, mirrored ceiling above. Slowly, luxuriously, I pulled the shopping bag across the crumpled sheets. Never taking my eyes from the deliciously drowsy and contented face, I pulled out a loaf of French bread and some rosy slices of roast beef. In a manner not dissimilar to that in which I had removed his shirt two hours before, I ripped off a goodly chunk of the crusty bread and piled the cool meat against it. Opened a brand new bottle of Newman's Own and began to pour it on the sandwich—in progress—when I was suddenly aware of a brightening sheen on my boyfriend's ribs and stomach. Yes! The bottle-neck is so wide that the savory mix of oils and spices had rushed out of the bottle in an uncontrolled torrent, soaked clean through the bread, and leaked onto my boyfriend's bare skin.

If you can't narrow your bottleneck, could you at least introduce to your otherwise finely packaged product one of those plastic doodads that restrict the stream to a sort of blop-blop-blop? It would make things ever so much easier for people in my position. I am

Very faithfully yours,
J.M.
San Diego, CA

The good thing about excesses is that

you can't get too much of them.

—STOLEN FROM
AN UNKNOWN POET
BY P. L. NEWMAN, 1985

☞ Cartoonists around the country began to feature our salad dressing in their cartoons, which accentuated our irreverent nature. Paul appeared on several interview programs, most notably with Gene Shalit on the *Today* show when Gene, on camera, pulled a head of lettuce out of his leather bag, Paul sprinkled it with the dressing, and they both chomped on it. Hotch wrote articles about the business for national publications. We also received wide coverage from the Associated Press and syndicated columnists. But more important, the buyers for the big chains were singing our praises. Dick Ponte, vice president of grocery procurement for Stop & Shop, said that "the dressing's success rests not in Mr. Newman's name or the company's nonprofit status, but in the taste. It's different from other salad dressings and it's high quality. People buy it for the same reason they buy other products. They like it." Michael Rourke, A&P vice president for marketing and corporate affairs, said, "Consumers won't buy an image twice. They have to like it. And the salad dressing has had success in getting good customer reaction to the product itself. As for advertising, strong public relations, which they have, can compensate for lack of advertising, and they've had tremendous publicity. With all those TV interviews and articles and columns written by food editors—that's the kind of publicity that's worth more than all the advertising dollars Newman could possibly spend."

The sales graph we had hung on the wall of our office, indicating sales from June to January, had gone off the chart by the first of November and was headed up the wall. By January it was starting across the ceiling.

☛ As Newman's Own began to grow by leaps and bounds, so did Ken's. Originally their little plant occupied thirteen thousand square feet, and they rented a forty-thousand-square-foot warehouse. But to keep up with the fast-growing demands of Newman's Own, Crowley had to make megaleaps of speed and, later, size. In the beginning, they were doing 60 bottles a minute, and then they went to 120, and then, in 1985, they built a new plant in Marlborough, Massachusetts, which upped the rate to 180 bottles a minute. Today, in their extended, improved plant, they are able to turn out Newman's Own at 400 bottles a minute. From a regular eight-hour-a-day business, they eventually had to go into three shifts trying to keep up with the Newman's Own demand. Screwed by our excellence, Ken's, with the profits they made from Newman's Own, has been able to extend their line of salad dressings so that now their products are in as many markets as Newman's Own. Even though they are competing on the same shelves, they continue to bottle the Newman's Own dressings, and the two companies maintain allegiances to each other.

Dear Mr. Newman:

I wish to commend and compliment you on the excellence and versatility of your salad dressing Newman's Own Oil & Vinegar Dressing. . . . The other day, I took a walk on the beach during my lunch hour, which is how I normally spend my lunches. This was preceded by a light but satisfying meal of a green salad topped by your special concoction, Newman's Own Olive Oil and Vinegar Salad Dressing. As I was saying, I took a walk on the beach, in the fine city of Solana Beach, and the only proper way to walk on the beach is to go barefoot . . .

When I got back to work, still barefoot, I noticed a large patch of tar, which I had apparently stepped on while walking. . . . Well, Mr. Newman (may I call you Paul?), I remembered my lunch, and your fine-tasting oil and vinegar dressing—and you know what, it really did the trick! Two applications of Newman's Own to the bottom of my foot really cut through the grease and grime and took that tar patch right off, baby. Not only is your product a treat for the palate, but it's also a great cleaning agent—and biodegradable too—truly a product for all seasons.

Most Sincerely,
K.J.
Oceanside, CA

CHAPTER

13

Whereas the salad dressing was the creation of a couple of merry pranksters, a happy accident, the pasta sauce was a deliberate vendetta, Paul's revenge against an offensive bottle of spaghetti sauce, or so the legend goes. Having returned to his Connecticut home one night, he found the house deserted, nothing in the kitchen to assuage his hunger save a lone jar of store-bought pasta sauce lurking in the corner of the cupboard next to a package of spaghetti, which he threw into a pot of boiling water. He dumped the sauce into a pan, swirled the spaghetti into it, and dug in, but one mouthful and his appetite went south. Bitter tomato taste full of sugar, chemical preservatives, phony coloring, as awful as those jars of salad dressing we first sampled—a spaghetti sauce that looked like red crankcase oil.

Paul decided right then and there that we needed to rescue the pasta eaters of the world with a new product, a sauce with whole chunks of vegetables and no phony preservatives or coloring or any of the other disgusting gunk that was buried in there.

When we went to the supermarket and got jars of all the sauces on the shelves, we found that, without exception, they were bland, tasteless, sweet, and terrible. We knew from our salad dressing experience that we now had to find a small, independent outfit that could bottle the kind of sauce we had in mind. We also knew how difficult that would be.

We cooked up a sauce in Paul's kitchen that contained tomato puree, tomato chunks, red and green peppers, celery, mushrooms, olive oil, spices, onion, garlic, all of it fresh, a chunky look to it, and Paul dashed off a legend to put on the bottle that told it the way it was:

Working 12 hour days . . . wrecked . . . hungry . . . arrive home, deserted by wife and children . . . cursing! Scan the cupboard—one package spaghetti—one bottle marinara sauce—run to the kitchen, cook—junk! YUK! Lie down, snooze . . . visions of culinary delights . . . Venetian ancestor tickles my ear, tickle, tickle . . . sauce talk . . . MAMA MIA! Dash to the vegetable patch . . . Yum yum . . . boil water . . . activate spaghetti . . . ditto the sauce . . . slurp, slurp . . . Terrifico! Magnifico! Slurp! Caramba! Bottle the sauce! . . . share with guys on street car . . . ah, me, finally immortal!

—P. Loquesto Newman

We now needed a name for this sauce, and what we came up with—Newman's Own Industrial Strength All-natural Venetian-style Spaghetti Sauce—horrified our brokers.

"Industrial strength! They'll think it's for factories—they'll never buy it to put on spaghetti." As usual, we disregarded their "expertise" and told Kalman to concentrate on finding a small company to bottle the sauce.

Fortuitously, Kalman's firm represented a small sauce producer in Rochester, New York, the Cantisano Company. Ralph Cantisano was an Italian sauce maker of the old school who in his kitchen had created Ragú, which eventually had become the best-selling sauce in the country. Cantisano had sold Ragú to Chesebrough-Pond's for a hefty sum and maintained this little plant in Rochester simply as a means of keeping his fine Italian hand in the pasta business.

Unfortunately, on the day Kalman met with Edward Salzano, Cantisano's executive vice president, to induce him to bottle our sauce, Salzano had summoned Kalman for the express purpose of firing him. Trying desperately to stave off the ax, Kalman plunked a bottle of our salad dressing on Salzano's desk and said, "You see this? This is Newman's Own, it's the best thing on the shelf, and we're selling the crap out of it. Now they want to create a spaghetti sauce, and if you guys can make up their sauce, we can make a deal with you."

Distracted from firing him, Salzano took the recipe Kalman gave him and turned it over to John LiDestri, who was CEO of Cantisano. It was a recipe like nothing they had ever seen before, nor had anyone else in the spaghetti sauce business. When Ralph Cantisano saw the recipe, he had serious doubts that a sauce with fresh components and no preservatives would have the necessary shelf life, the same doubts that we had encountered with our dressing and that we would face with all our natural products, primarily because no one had ever bottled fresh stuff before without fixing it with chemical preservatives. In addition, Cantisano had a negative attitude about personality foods. He had been approached by many Italian celebrities at one time or another, Dean Martin, Frank Sinatra, Dom DeLuise, Connie Francis, Rocky Graziano, but all these people wanted him to manufacture their sauces and pay them a license fee. Since the Newman's Own situation was different in that they were going to purchase the product and sell it themselves, and although skeptical about this movie star and writer who had drummed up a sauce with fresh ingredients, Cantisano told LiDestri to meet with us.

When LiDestri came to our office in Westport, he was taken aback by that prominent wall sign: THERE ARE THREE RULES FOR RUNNING A BUSINESS: FORTUNATELY, WE DON'T KNOW ANY OF THEM.

LiDestri says, "I was rather discouraged when I discovered that Paul and Hotch had no marketing survey, no business plan, no budget, no organized strategy for the introduction of the sauce. When I asked about this lack of preparation, the haphazard nature of their business, Paul said, 'Me in this business is just part of life's great folly. Stay loose, men, keep 'em off balance.' "

"Do you guys realize that with this recipe of yours you are attempting to revolutionize the spaghetti sauce industry? Every sauce on the market, including the one we make, is a puree-type product, the better ones tomato based. Most of them are made with modified food starch to thicken them. There isn't a single product that has any particulates in it—by that I mean you won't find chunks of tomato or pieces of mushrooms or anything else that is identifiable. If the sauce is a mushroom sauce, the pieces of mushrooms are minuscule specks. Spaghetti sauce is purchased as a base to be doctored up in the home kitchen by adding mushrooms, onions, a little wine, sugar, meat if desired—it's really a homemade sauce, using the jar sauce as the base. All of us spaghetti sauce manufacturers believe that if you show any particulates in the sauce, even seeds, it would turn off the customers.

"So you're asking us to invest our company money and time to gamble on shelf life, which it very likely won't have, on housewives buying chunky sauces, which they probably won't, and on a business that gives all of its capital away in December and in January has to borrow money from the bank to start the new year, a company with no business plan or budget. That's it, isn't it?"

We said, "Yep."

"Don't you think you'd be better off bringing out a traditional sauce and eliminate the risk factors?"

We said, "Nope."

☛ As it turned out, duplicating our kitchen sauce in the Cantisano factory was even more difficult than it had been for the salad dressing. Dozens of trial bottles traveled between Rochester and Westport, each one of them dutifully sampled by us; but getting the proper taste balance among the elements in the bottle proved to be very tricky. Too much oregano, or not enough onion, the consistency of the tomatoes—the two bumbling amateurs from Connecticut were driving the professionals in Rochester nuts.

Also driving the Cantisano contingent batty was the problem of how to fill the jars with our chunky contents using machinery that was designed for smooth-flowing sauce; even more of a problem was how to cook in kettles that were made for puree and not for particulates. In both cases, new equipment had to be designed. Larger valves replaced the smaller ones that would have restricted the flow of the contents into the jars.

As for the cooking process, we were told that our recipe couldn't be mixed in the existing vats, which used big corkscrew mixers to pulverize the contents. They worked like a Waring blender, a shaft down the center of a big vat that whirled and whipped up the contents into a smooth sauce. Of course, that wouldn't work for our sauce, thereby creating a critical situation in our relations with Cantisano. To cook our sauce, they would have to devise new kettles with a very soft side-sweep agitation, insuring that the chunky stuff on the bottom, by the natural weight of it, would not be squashed. Everything had to be suspended in constant movement.

Obviously, all this would entail a considerable capital investment for equipment, which at that time could be used only for our untested product. It was a stand-off, a matter of who would blink first. Would Cantisano make the investment? Would we settle for a puree-type content?

Cantisano blinked.

At that very moment, we were about to introduce our salad dressing to the West Coast with a launch party in Los Angeles. Although our spaghetti sauce was not yet in production, we arranged for graphic artists to make 120 handmade labels and for the now approved sauce to be produced in the Cantisano kitchen in time for twenty cases to be shipped to Los Angeles for the launching. The bottles were hand-filled in the Cantisano kitchen, and as a result, the food critics at the Hollywood launch sampled chunky marinara sauce from out of a jar for the first time ever. The overall reaction was favorable, and with their cooking kettles now adapted for the new contents, Cantisano went into production.

"Back then," Salzano recalls, "the run time was slow. There really weren't any high-speed manufacturers. It would have been unthinkable to have to turn out two million cases a year, so actually we grew and learned as Newman's Own was growing and learning. The first two items that we produced were the Industrial Strength Marinara and the Mushroom Marinara, then the Sockarooni, and then one after the other the more complicated spaghetti sauces. That Newman's Own gave away all its profits to charity was beginning to receive meaningful publicity. That a movie superstar and a best-selling author were singing wacko songs about their product captured a lot of space because these were not a couple of guys who were self-serving, chest-beating individuals. The eating public liked them, liked their products, and liked their generosity."

The second product Cantisano packed for us began with a little round bottle covered in Styrofoam that we thought would be a perfect receptacle for salsa. LiDestri mocked up a few bottles and brought them to the Newman's Own Christmas party that year, where everyone gave it a thumbs-up. We decided it was a perfect fit for our string of spaghetti sauces.

"In the meantime," LiDestri says, "we were reinvesting our profits into our business, enabling us to build a new factory and to increase the number of jars from one hundred twenty-five a minute to today's machinery, which runs six hundred jars a minute. We now have three hundred employees and a busy West Coast operation that supplies Newman's Own spaghetti sauces and salsas to the entire western part of the United States.

"In retrospect, I think what really helped us develop products was the fact that we had a Paul Newman and A. E. Hotchner available to taste each rendition right then and there and render an opinion. The dynamics of that was so unique, it made it possible finally to turn out a product that satisfied them. People would say to me, 'Is Newman really involved in this thing?' and they were surprised to hear that no product ever goes out unless he personally eats it, and if he doesn't like it, it's not going any-place. Hotchner and Newman were hands-on about everything. They wrote the legends, they tinkered with the label, they were thoroughly involved. If ever there was a personal, intimate busi-ness, this was it.

"I guess you could say that Paul Newman's hunger that night in Westport revolutionized spaghetti eating in America."

Dear Mr. Newman:

I would like to take this opportunity to thank you for saving my dog's life. I realize this is an unusual statement writing to a food company which aims its products at humans, but your Sockarooni spaghetti sauce did in fact save my dog.

Charlie is a nine-year-old Welsh terrier who suffered a se-vere bout of pancreatitis in December and was put on a strict medicated dog food diet by the vet. It was a low-fat diet, since I guess his pancreas has trouble digesting high fat foods. To make a long story shorter, he had a relapse in July when he and the raccoons got into the garbage. This happened while we were on vacation and our housesitter did not realize he was not eat-ing his food.

When we returned from vacation, he was so thin you could see every bone in his body, so back to the vet and IV's we went. After several days, the vet sent him home and told me to do the best I could with trying to get him to eat. No luck.

That night my husband and I were having Sockarooni spaghetti sauce and Charlie seemed interested in the aromas. We figured we had nothing to lose, and let him lick the pan. He cleaned the pan and then sat up and begged for more. For the next week he ate Newman's Own Sockarooni mixed with rice and a little dog food kibble. Gradually, he regained his strength and returned to his normal diet. When I tell people about the incident, yes, they do say, "It has gone to the dogs," but I don't care. It sure is cheaper than the vet bills, or putting a dog down!

C.G.
Saratoga, CA

CHAPTER 14

This time to give a boost start to our fledgling spaghetti sauce, we made plans to stage a festive media party at Keen's Chop House in Manhattan, not a glamorous spot by any means but suited to the bizarre nature of our company. The media turnout exceeded the Hanratty's introduction of the salad dressing, and with the cameras rolling, Paul and Joanne sang the praises of the spaghetti sauce in songs that Hotch brazenly composed to the music of Frederick Loewe and George Gershwin, both of whom would have been horrified:

(To the tune of Loewe's "I've Grown Accustomed to Her Face")

PAUL:
I've tasted sauces from the East,
Some made with curdled milk and yeast,
And the spaghetti drenched with grease
That makes you so obese,
It sticks to you,
And tastes like glue,
Those pasta sauces on the shelf,

No self-respecting man would eat.
I have Italian blood that needs a good spaghetti now
     and then,
Malnutrition almost drove me round the bend—
That's when . . .

There came to me while deep in sleep,
A recipe divine,
A recipe that's mine. . . .

(To the tune of Gershwin's "I've Got Rhythm")

JOANNE:
It's got onions,
It's got garlic,
It's got basil,
Who could ask for anything more?

It's got olive
Oil and spices,
It's all nat'ral,
True industrial strength galore!

Pride of Venice,
Rome and Pisa,
It'sa sure that
It'll please ya.

Lots of peppers,
Fresh tomatoes,

Cup of sunshine,
Who could ask for anything more?
Who could ask for anything more?

PAUL:
I'm as content as I can be,
That now I have a spaghetti,
Of which my ancestors can be
So justly proud of me—
From Sha-ker Heights,
To Ve-nice nights.
And now Andretti says that he,
Would like to give me the Grand Prix,
For having fin'lly made a sauce
That's like he had in Italy,
He then ran a vic'try lap for him and me,
You see . . .

If you will keep on buying them,
It will become a fact,
Newman won't have to act!

JOANNE AND PAUL:
Who could ask for anything more?
Who could ask for anything more?

Keen's kitchen produced a variety of pastas, all anointed with our Industrial Strength elixir, on serving platters scattered around the restaurant. The bar flowed freely while scores of photographers and TV cameramen recorded the event, which appeared

on the evening's news channels and in syndicated newspaper articles. Supermarket executives were more numerous than at the
Hanratty's event, and the following day our brokers were overwhelmed with orders. The food industry (or any other) had
never seen an introductory promotion quite like this, nor had
they seen the chunky, all-natural product we were promoting.

A month later, we repeated the spaghetti sauce event in Los
Angeles at a hamburger restaurant in Burbank owned by Paul's
friend Ron Buck. For this occasion we added the composer
Henry Mancini, who accompanied Joanne and Paul when they
sang the spaghetti sauce song.

CHAPTER 15

We were beginning to learn the food ropes, when to say yes, when to say no (and mean it), and, since we were inevitably going to make mistakes, how to avoid fatal ones. One of the first things we learned was that in the war for shelf space in the supermarkets, a lone bottle of Newman's Own Salad Dressing would get overwhelmed by the army of Kraft bottles and others with multifacings. Same held true for a lone bottle of Industrial Strength Marinara up against the rows of Ragú, Prego, and Progresso. So we created troops to reinforce the embattled solo Industrial Strength. Mushroom Marinara hit the shelves and then Sockarooni, with a blend of tomatoes, peppers, and spices, and bearing the following legend:

> Sockarooni/Sock-it-to'em Spaghetti Sauce all alone, by itself, just sitting there naked, will blow your socks off! Take yourself back to 1833 when Neapolitan adventurers in St. Louis concocted this specific sauce, ingesting same, gathering strength, courage, endurance and wit to wrassle 1000 pound

> bears. 150 years later I fortify myself with
> Sockarooni to wrassle my own private bear—which
> is "jist gittin' through the day."
>
> —P. Loquesto Newman

Once again the doom-and-gloom brokers, not having learned their lesson from Industrial Strength, warned us that a sauce named Sockarooni would never get to the checkout counter, and once again they were dead wrong. Sockarooni captured the fancy of those who liked spicy hunks of peppers and tomatoes and those people who enjoyed having their socks blown off.

We continued building up our troops with Bombolina (tomato and fresh basil), and this time there wasn't a peep out of the brokers.

We also enlisted additional salad dressings, one of which was our Family Recipe Italian with this legend on the back of the bottle:

> In 1499 the fierce Gelato clan of northern Italy
> and the bellicose Viagrani Nooni clan of the south
> engaged in the now famous Salad Dressing War,
> each side claiming their dressing was superior.
> After 10 years of intermittent salad-tossing and
> some cross-dressing, Cardinal Newmanelli the Just
> brought the warring factions to the table and
> mediated a salad dressing combining the best
> features of both. For two centuries this combination
> was the official family dressing for all Italy. Then,

during the Great Prosciutto War of 1710, the
recipe went poof, lost, until recently, when it was
unearthed in a decrepit palazzo on the Gran
Canal. The magical recipe recipeared so to speak,
and is finally the dressing that united Italy.

—P. Loquesto Newman

But in the course of churning out new products, we came per-
ilously close to putting ourselves out of business because we
hadn't taken into account a new phenomenon in the food business, a diabolical supermarket invention—slotting. If ever there
was a dirty word in the food business, slotting is it. Competition
for shelf space had always been intense, and products were selected at the whim of the supermarket buyer. Some traditional
emoluments were involved in getting a new product on the shelf,
like giving one free bottle for every ten purchased or offering an
introductory promotion—we would lower the price and pass the
savings on to the consumer, who instead of buying one jar for
$1.99 would buy two jars at $1.59; the extra sales generated by the
promotion would make up for the price reduction. But slotting
involved actual cash payments of $28,000–$30,000 to each store
for the privilege of displaying a new product, and there was no
guarantee as to how long a store would keep it on the shelf. Thus,
if you simultaneously introduced two new products in twelve different markets, you would have to pony up as much as $400,000.

Unlike some of the other immature ventures that foundered
and sank under the bombardment of slotting, we flourished, and
in a relatively short time we had a platoon of Newman's Own
pasta sauces attacking the shelf spaces.

> ROASTED GARLIC & PEPPERS
>
> Once upon a time, in the darkest of ages, there lived a green grocer named Newmadnezzer, who was famed for his virile garlic and voluptuous peppers. One starlit night, the Prince of the Garlic Bin climbed the fence and courted Princess Gwen Pepper in a heated mating dance that lasted a fortnight and wound up with a royal nuptial. A month later, as noted in the Baby Book of Records, Princess Gwen became the first stuffed pepper. It is her progeny who have danced their way into this bottle and onto your pasta.
>
> —Newt Newmadnezzer, XVI

We were also augmenting our salad dressing troops but spacing them to avoid falling into the slotting trap.

Sales for our first six months were $502,000 with a profit of $65,000, which we distributed to our first charities. In 1983, our first full year in business, our sales catapulted to $3,204,335, with a profit of $397,000, which we dispensed to scores of different charities. In June of that year, when time came for Joanne to open their swimming pool and she couldn't find the outdoor furniture, Paul told her to replace everything because it looked as though we were going to last longer than expected. By the end of 1984, when sales had quadrupled to $11,943,976 and we had sold 18,705,555 bottles of salad dressing and 8,371,726 jars of spaghetti sauce, enabling us to give away $2,023,105, we knew we were in for a long and fruitful haul.

☛ It is 1989, and Frank Sinatra is holding a press conference in a Los Angeles restaurant with his Rat Pack buddies present (Dean Martin, Peter Lawford, Sammy Davis Jr.) to announce to a packed media audience that he is throwing his celebrated snap-brim fedora into the food ring, challenging Paul Newman with his very own spaghetti sauce, four different varieties. Frank announces that he has formed a limited partnership called Artanis Foods (Sinatra spelled backward) to license his spaghetti sauces and that Armanino Foods of Distinction, Inc., of San Francisco holds the license to market and operate the Artanis Company.

A reporter asks, "Will you be going into the Artanis office to run the business?"

"Well," Frank says, "we don't have an office. We'll be operating out of the Armanino office."

"Will you be going in there to handle things?"

"Yeah, I'll be around, but Bill Armanino here will be running the business."

"Frank, why are you going into the spaghetti sauce business?"

"I like seeing my name on all those bottles in the supermarket."

"You know, Mr. Sinatra, Tommy Lasorda had a spaghetti sauce and it went belly-up."

"Yeah, well, Tommy spent too much time in the dugout and not enough in the kitchen."

"Frank, can you tell us your recipe?"

"Sure. First you start with some olive oil and some garlic, four whole cloves. You heat the oil and add the garlic. Puncture the garlic with an ordinary fork so it exudes the flavor. When the garlic turns tan, turn off the oil and throw it out. Save the oil. Next, you take two whole cans of the Italian plum tomatoes.

Place the can in the blender and count to a slow four. Put the tomatoes into a large saucepan. Add some basil, salt, pepper, oregano, and the oil. Bring the sauce to a boil. Skim the oil that rises to the top. Dip a piece of bread in the sauce, testing to see when the sauce is finished. At the end you might want to add some fresh parsley. And there you have it—the Sinatra special."

"How you gonna do all that on an assembly line?"

"How the hell do I know? That's Bill Armanino's job."

"Frank, do you think your spaghetti sauce will do better than the Frank Sinatra neckties that came out a couple of years ago and tanked?"

"You bet. My sauce will be going down the throat, not around it."

"Mr. Sinatra, how is your product different from Paul Newman's?"

"Well, two ways: I am a legit Italian with spaghetti sauce in my blood, whereas Newman is an obvious outsider. And besides, Newman gives all his profits to charity, but all my profits will be going into my pocket."

☞ It is April 1992, and William Armanino has called a press conference to announce the demise of Sinatra's spaghetti sauce, reporting a "substantial loss" ($229,000 for the last quarter) for the Artanis partnership. Obviously no profits ever found their way into Frank's pocket. Marketing analyst Dan Swander said, "If you stop and think about it, what does Sinatra have to do with pasta sauce? Maybe people can get carried away with the romance, but when you step back and think why do people buy pasta sauce—it's because they're looking for a quality product, not whose name's on it."

Another analyst said: "The Sinatra sauce was mediocre, rather bland, whereas a jar of Newman's delivers something special. That's why one flopped and the other didn't."

John Owen, a food critic and columnist, had this appraisal: "It sounded like a good idea when Ol' Blue Eyes decided to bottle up his four favorite styles of pasta sauce. After all, Paul Newman has banked a small fortune (for charitable projects) from his brands of dressings and sauces. But I suspect Sinatra was not given a standing ovation by supermarket shoppers because for years, he was identified as the leader of the Rat Pack. Admit it. That is not a label you are immediately inclined to slap on a jug of pasta sauce. And when Sinatra was hitting all the Las Vegas nightspots with Dean Martin, Peter Lawford and Sammy Davis, Jr., newspaper photos invariably showed them with drinks in their hands and showgirls perched on their laps.

"Maybe we formed inaccurate stereotypes, but it was difficult to imagine Sinatra in a 'Danger, Genius at Work' apron, slaving over a stove in his test kitchen, adding a pinch of oregano here and a dash of basil there.

"Paul Newman? Maybe. I've always suspected that his wife, Joanne Woodward, kept him pretty much in line. I wouldn't be surprised to hear he carries out the garbage and waters the plants when she's away on location."

☞ In 1993, Paul's daughter Nell, in partnership with a friend of hers who had been in the swimming pool business, proposed that they create an organic food subsidiary of Newman's Own. Paul agreed to finance them for a year so that they could educate themselves; they used that time to do extensive research on the possibility of coming out with products for the snack food market that were all organic. They decided on organic pretzels as their first product. In no time, they became the dominant player in this small market, which was confined largely to health food stores. They next produced organic chocolate bars in six flavors, soon followed by a variety of organic cookies, one of which was called Fig Newmans. The Fig Newman was launched in 1998, and sales for the first seven months were $751,000. All together, sales for that period amounted to $1.3 million. Tortilla chips and popcorn have joined the roster. Late in 2001, Organics, now solid enough to stand on its own, became an independent company that also gives its profits—now totaling $2.75 million—to charity.

Mr. Newman:

Last night my girlfriend treated me to a fabulous meal. It was quick and easy and quite good.

It consisted of spaghetti and green salad using your brand. All we did was pour your spaghetti sauce over pasta and make a tossed salad with your dressing. No fuss and very tasty. There's nothing to add so you can see why it was Q&E.

During dinner, my girlfriend mentioned you were a movie star. I would be interested to know what you've made. If you act as well as you cook, your movies would be worth watching.

Keep up the good work,

M.A.
Ranch Cordova, CA
P.S. Are any of your movies in VCR?

Dear Mr. Newman:

My 92-year-old dad likes popcorn, but has had to give it up because of the hull getting under his dentures. I gave him a handful of your popcorn and the first bite was followed by "Hey, that melts in your mouth." Took out his dentures and showed me—clean as a whistle.

> W.S.
> Danger, TX

Dear Col. "Pops" Newman . . .

Bought your popcorn because I hate the looks of that *&#N@%*&# ricki-dicki, Orville what's his face . . . ? Anyway, it is very good. Do you realize that the easiest way to make popcorn is not in one of those bulky corn-poppers, but in a Chinese wok? I just put a little oil in the bottom, heat it, add a cup of popcorn, shake it easily a few times and glorious popcorn! No fuss, no bother!

Anyway, it sure is nice to see a decent face on the popcorn label and not that saber-toothed male hag and his equally goofy grandson!

> Sincerely,
> M.S.
> Seattle, WA

CHAPTER

16

We are in the kitchen of a rented house in Fort Lauderdale, Florida, where Paul is directing and acting in *Harry and Son*. It's the fourth time Hotch has flown in from New York bearing popcorn samples. On previous visits, he has brought red kernels and black kernels, kernels from Iowa, Nebraska, Kansas, Texas, and Rhode Island, but none has satisfied Paul's finicky popcorn palate. Beer and popcorn have been lifelong staples of his diet, and whatever kernel is now going to fly the Newman's Own banner, it just better outpop what Orville Redenbacher has on his shelf, a popcorn that Paul considers an insult to popcorn aficionados. For two years Paul and Hotch have been searching for the ultimate kernel. The usual tasting process on these *Harry and Son* occasions is to pop up a batch in the kitchen hot-air popper and invite the cast and crew for a communal tasting (microwave won't appear for another two years). Ellen Barkin, who is in *Harry*, matches Paul in her popcorn avidity.

What we are now tasting is a hybrid kernel grown by the Wyandot Company of Canton, Ohio, developed specifically to meet Paul's exacting requirements. The aroma is felicitous, and the kernels pop large and tender. Paul flicks melted butter and salt over the popcorn, and the sound of untidy lip smacking and teeth clacking fills the kitchen. "Wow!" says Hotch. "Better than sex!" Ellen gives him a look. "Well," he amends lamely, "almost as good." No one disagrees.

When we get back to New York, Wyandot sends us four variations of that hybrid kernel, each with a different moisture content. They are popped separately and put in bowls. Paul is blindfolded. He carefully samples each variety, sipping beer in between, then finally makes a choice, and that becomes our third product: Newman's Own Old Style Picture Show Popcorn, with this legend on the back of the bottle:

I'll tell you how bad it is. Nobody gets trusted with popcorn—except me. That includes the FBI, the IRS, Tiffany's and concessionaires of any ilk. A good flick arrives on the local screen, you see ol' Newman scuttling across the lobby with a greasy brown paper bag of this homemade popcorn in one hand and—you guessed it—a machete in the other. Who's who lists a lot of one-armed people in my hometown. They got caught trying to muscle their way into my greasy brown paper bag. The way I feel—they got off easy. They should have been strung up.

—Col. P. L. "Pops" Newman

To bring this cataclysmic event to the attention of the world, we schedule a popcorn pop-off on the grounds of the Westport Historical Society, everyone dressed in old-style costumes circa the 1880s. A madcap Dixieland band plays for the unveiling, and Paul once more courageously sings, this time Hotch's popcorn song, which again abuses Gilbert & Sullivan's "I Am the Very Model of a Modern Major-General."

We gave the world a salad dressing that is truly magnifique,
And then a marinara sauce gourmet Italians call unique,
And now we bring you popcorn with a lot of special properties,
The connoisseurs have all agreed we have produced a crop to
*   please.*

Our popcorn makes you smile when you are suffering dyspepsia,
And it will goose your appetite when you have anorexia.
And all the horny Englishmen and Finns and overzealous
*   Czechs,*
Will find that Newman's Own is better than the kinkiest of sex!

CHORUS:
The good news is that Newman's Own is better than the kinkiest
*   of sex!*
The good news is that Newman's Own is better than the kinkiest
*   of sex!*
The good news is that Newman's Own is better than the kinkiest
*   of sex!*

To find a popcorn oo-là-là we searched through several
*   continents,*
To find the one that had the most extraordinary redolence,
In Turkey, Spain, Iran, Iraq, we searched for popcorn high and
*   low,*
How the hell were we to know we'd find it in Ohi-i-o!

It is the color of the sun and pops as white as falling snow,
And if your car should ever stall our hot popcorn will make it go,
The lights are low, your girl says no, and you are really through
*   unless,*
You feed her full of Newman's Own and turn her no into a yes!

CHORUS:
You feed her full of Newman's Own and turn her no into a yes!
You feed her full of Newman's Own and turn her no into a yes!
You feed her full of Newman's Own and turn her no into a
*   ye-e-es!*

Our blend of corn will most assuredly promote good fellowship,
And ev'rything is natural to clear up gout and nasal drip!
And now we tell you finally with candor and with clarity,
That you should buy a lot because our profits go to charity!

☛ At our popcorn event, Paul and Hotch officiated over the wine bar; Hotch filled each glass, which he handed to Paul, who in turn handed it to the guest. One lady, adoration in her eyes, asked Paul to stir the drink with his finger before handing it to her. "Ice cubes are safer," said PL. Another lady asked him if he would remove his sunglasses so she could gaze at his celebrated blue eyes. "I'd be glad to, madame," he said, "but I think it would make my pants fall down."

Over the years, popcorn has brought Paul some unanticipated perks, like the night he was going considerably over the speed limit and got pulled over by a police cruiser. The officer came over, asked for Paul's driver's license, got out a ticket, and started to write but stopped when he looked at Paul's license, looked in at him, did a kind of ritual dance around the car, slapping his leg and muttering, "I can't believe it, I can't believe it." Then he said, "What'll I tell my wife? That I arrested Paul Newman? Take off. My God, we eat your popcorn every night."

Today there's an entire generation that knows Paul more for popcorn than for movies. An interviewer recently asked him the secret of his success. Paul said, "I don't have the slightest idea. We have no plan. We have never had a plan. Hotch and I comprise two of the great witless people in business—none of this is supposed to work, you understand. We are a testament to the theory of Random—whatever that means!"

☞ We are in the Newman kitchen, where Joanne has invited us to sample something she has concocted. Until now, Joanne has been amused and impressed by us, more observer than participant, but now she places glasses in front of us and fills them from a pitcher containing a golden liquid. It is, quite simply, the best lemonade we have ever tasted. She has decided to let Newman's Own in on the secret recipe that has been guarded zealously by seven generations of her Georgia family. Right then and there we decide on its name: Newman's Own Old Fashioned Roadside Virgin Lemonade. Joanne questions the validity of "virgin," and we explain that the lemons that will be used will have never been squeezed before. We also have the gall to proclaim, "It restores virginity." The legend we concoct gives Joanne full credit for what will become an instant winner at the refrigerated fresh drink section of the country's supermarkets:

The marathon in Africa . . . I'm halfway out and
barely chugging. Mountain coming! Liquid needed!
What's around? Water's bitter! Beer's flat! Gator,
Blah Blah! . . . Fading fast. Then a vision—sweet
Joanna!—tempting me with pale gold nectar . . .
lemon is it? By golly! Lemonade? No, Lemon
Aid! . . . Power added! Asphalt churning . . .
Cruising home to victory! Hail Joanna! Filched the
nectar (shameless hustler!)—In the market—
Newman's Own!

—Paul Newman

We enlist Whoopi Goldberg for the lemonade poster, and the
photo shoot is an event of unrelieved hilarity as Whoopi,
dressed in a virginal gown, is kneeling on a blue silk pillow at the
base of a waterfall while Paul, in his Butch Cassidy getup, his
red-stockinged feet in a pool of water, pours the lemonade into
a chalice Whoopi is holding while she mutters swooningly, "I
can feel it! I can feel it! It's being restored! I'm becoming a
virgin! Yes, yes, I'm a virgin again!"

A broad ribbon, supported by white doves, runs across her mid-
section, carrying the boldly lettered words *RESTORES VIRGINITY!*

We are happy to report that we have never been challenged
by the truth-in-advertising people—in fact, we have received
testimonials like this:

Dear Mr. Newman:

We each bought a carton of your Newman's Own Old

Fashioned Roadside Virgin Lemonade. It was very tasty and refreshing; however, we have a few questions:

1. Do you have to be a virgin to drink this lemonade or

2. Is the factory where it is produced run by virgins? If so, do you, Mr. Newman, personally certify that each worker is, in fact, a virgin? Does he/she have to be a virgin during the entire processing or can he/she be a virgin when first hired?

3. If the lemons are virgins, how can you tell? Perhaps a few promiscuous lemons sneak their way in. You know how it is with lemons. Would a quick squeeze disqualify the virgin lemons? Is it o.k. if they are a little tart?

This whole virgin business is confusing, however, we may be willing to work with other virgins in your factory if the price is right. Our husbands will certify that we are truly virgins.

Sincerely,
C.S.
D.N.
Delmar, NY

In a newspaper article, Paul was quoted as saying, "Joan Collins was restored to virginity after drinking four quarts of it, and Sylvester Stallone is on his forty-sixth case and still hoping." In another interview, Hotch was quoted as saying that the lemonade would probably become "the official drink of Planned Parenthood."

As new products spilled from the Newman's Own cornucopia—Microwave Popcorn; Light Italian Dressing; a Fra Diavolo sauce with a really spicy kick; a thick, full-bodied salsa with three degrees of heat; Ranch Dressing; Bombolina Pasta Sauce ("The Intimate Companion Your Pasta Will Never Forget"); Caesar Dressing, with Paul's marble bust on the label; Five Cheese Pasta Sauce (blue, Parmesan, Romano, Asiago, and provolone) called "Say Cheese"—on and on they marched to join the Newman's Own troops on the battlefield of the store shelves.

☛ From the get-go, we had a policy of not advertising because (1) we thought it was tacky, (2) we found it was not always productive, and (3) we couldn't afford the astronomically expensive campaigns to rival our giant competition. Felicitously, we were receiving a lot of unsolicited accolades: *Consumer Reports* rates Newman's Own Microwave Popcorn number one over a field of thirty brands, including Pop Secret, Orville Redenbacher, Act II, Jolly Time, and Jiffy Pop; we are given the Connecticut Governor's Laurel Award for responsible social involvement; *Los Angeles* magazine awards Newman's Own Microwave Popcorn four stars and says it "deserves a popping Oscar"; the Council on Economic Priorities bestows its Charitable Giving Award upon us; *USA Today* rates Newman's Own Popcorn number one; *Entertainment Weekly* calls us the "tops of the pops"; the *Boston Globe* labels our Marinara Pasta Sauce the "hit of the week"; our Light Italian Dressing is rated against forty-six brands of low-calorie dressings, including Wishbone, Kraft, Hidden Valley, Seven Seas, and Marzetti's Thousand Island, and declared "Best of the Bottled Dressing . . . our hands-down favorite" by *McCall's* food editors; the Food and Beverage Marketing New Product Review awards Newman's Own Salsa a top rating of two and a half stars out of three—"This product is fun and tasty too"; the *Sacramento Bee* stages a popcorn contest and declares our Butter-Flavored Microwave Popcorn "the clear winner over Jolly Time, Pop Secret, Orville Redenbacher, Pop 'n Snack, and others . . . Perfect crunch, melts in your mouth, makes you want more"; the *San Francisco Chronicle*'s Hot Stuff Awards rates Newman's Own All Natural Bandito Salsa above its eight competitors; the *New York Times* names Newman's Own "the preferred brand" in a tasting of sixteen marinara sauces, including Progresso, Contadina, Rao's, Aunt Millie's, Buitoni, Francesco Rinaldi, Enrico, Prego, and Ragú, by Florence Fabricant, the chief food critic; the *Sacramento Bee*'s six judges sample twelve national brands of chunky red salsa and rate Newman's Own at the top; our salsa also wins the *Burlington Times* taste test, where it is called "a salsa for all seasons"; *USA Today* asks the celebrated Italian cook and author Mary Ann Esposito, who is host of PBS's *Ciao Italia*, to do a blind taste test of the nine leading marinara sauces, and Newman's Own emerges with the highest "3" rating, while Barilla, Francesco Rinaldi, Healthy Choice, Ragú, and Prego receive only a "1" rating, the lowest; the *Chicago Tribune* rates the six leading popcorns, with Newman's Own described as "the perfect all around popcorn with a mouthwatering buttery taste that isn't greasy, the pieces are big and crunchy, and it has just the right amount of salt. And the price is decent, too, so we rate it an A"—Pop Secret, Orville Redenbacher, and Act II get Bs, while Dominic's and Jewel get Ds; the *Reno Gazette-Journal* assembles a five-judge salsa panel that puts Newman's Own Salsa far out in front of such longtime salsas as Ortega and La Victoria; the *Centre Daily Times* also assembles a panel to judge salsa, and again we are the only ones to rate the coveted four peppers; the *Boston Herald*'s headline says it all—"FOR SALSA SELECTION, JUDGES SAY NEWMAN'S OWN IS HOT!"—which means that the five leading competitors are not so hot; *Consumer Reports* rates thirty-nine tomato-based sauces, and our Sockarooni scores above all our chief competitors— Contadina, Francesco Rinaldi, Ragú, Prego, Progresso, and Classico di Sicilia.

In addition to all these awards, there were awards of distinction: Paul and Hotch received Columbia University's Lawrence A. Wien Special Recognition Award for Outstanding Philanthropic Commitments; the Jean Hersholt Humanitarian Award Oscar was given to Paul for his "commitment to philanthropy"; Hotch collected the James Beard Humanitarian of the Year Award on Paul's behalf at its annual gala in New York.

We also benefited from news reports like this one, which was sent to newspapers nationwide by the PR Newswire:

Today, it was learned that a truck containing a shipment of Newman's Own salad dressing was stolen last week, while en route from Southern California to Portland, Oregon. Other brands of salad dressing were on the truck as well but were untouched. The truck has been recovered, but the Newman's Own salad dressing is still missing at this time. The missing product includes 664 cases of Olive Oil & Vinegar, 238 cases of Balsamic Vinaigrette, and 344 cases of Family Recipe Italian flavors. Law enforcement authorities are baffled.

When advised of the situation, Paul Newman said, "To be chosen and bought is one thing, to be stolen before all the others is a choice honor indeed. It's a great vote of confidence in our products, the other national brands of salad dressing must feel unwanted."

Little is known about the thieves, however the initial sense is they must be very discerning people because late last week, 4 cases of empty bottles of the missing products were returned to a local recycling center in Newport, Oregon. Upon learning of this, Mr. Newman commented, "They may be thieves, but at least they're environmentalists."

Not only were newspapers and magazines providing these unsolicited sales enhancers, but we were also benefiting from three events that were covered nationally. We had formed an entente with *Good Housekeeping* magazine (4,534,700 readers) to sponsor a recipe contest that required entrants to use a Newman's Own product in their submissions. But instead of the customary cash awards to the winners, we offered those winners emoluments to give to their favorite charities. When the contest was first announced in *Good Housekeeping*, the "experts" (the same negative bunch who had doubted us from the beginning) scoffed at a contest that did not offer cash prizes. The naysayers warned us that we would get very few entrants. As it turned out, however, the Newman's Own Charity Awards tapped the *Good Housekeeping* readers' innate desire to help causes they cared about, and our contest attracted a huge response, second only to the Pillsbury contest, which gave $1 million in cash to the winner. In our case, we gave $50,000 to the charity of the winner and $10,000 to four runners-up. The finalists were brought to New York from all over the United States, and at an elaborate luncheon, which we staged in Rockefeller Center's Rainbow Room complex, the winning recipes were served to Paul and

Joanne, who, before an audience that included food critics, television coverage, and supermarket executives, rated each dish as prepared and presented by a Rainbow Room chef (some of these winning recipes can be found in the appendix). All together, over the nine years the contest flourished, there were twenty thousand recipe submissions and $2 million distributed to the winners, who bestowed their largesse on such charities as Habitat for Humanity, the Special Olympics, Amnesty International, Child Abuse Prevention Effort, Multiple Sclerosis Society, the Starlight Foundation, and the Salvation Army.

A second yearly event that was consistently covered by the media was cosponsored by Newman's Own and John F. Kennedy Jr.'s *George* magazine. John and Paul both wanted to recognize corporate giving, and the George Award was created to honor the American company that best exemplified good citizenship through philanthropy, as demonstrated by monetary gifts or creative grassroots programs. A check for $250,000 was given to the charity of choice of the award recipient, who was chosen from hundreds of nominees by a selection committee like this one for the 1999 contest: Maya Angelou, Marvin Davis, Marian Wright Edelman, A. E. Hotchner, John F. Kennedy Jr., Philippe de Montebello, Paul Newman, General Norman Schwarzkopf, and Joanne Woodward. The $250,000 winner that year was Hal Taussig, president of Idyll, Ltd., a travel industry company that donated all its profits to the company's charitable foundation, which in turn funneled those funds into a low-interest lending program for individuals and small businesses to use for start-up costs. These borrowers had to adhere to the foundation's goal of creating jobs among the hard-core unemployed and assisting in low-cost housing in decaying urban centers.

The Newman's Own–George Awards were terminated upon the tragic death of John F. Kennedy Jr.

A third annual event that has received wide coverage in print and television is the First Amendment Prize, which we organized in partnership with PEN American Center. For the past ten years, the $25,000 prize has been awarded to a United States resident who has fought courageously, despite adversity, to safeguard the First Amendment right to freedom of expression as it applies to the written word. Ten years ago at the initial press conference announcing the award, Paul said: "One of the basic guarantees of the Bill of Rights is freedom of the press, freedom to write and publish without any abridgment. It is to safeguard and promote that freedom that we have established this award. To paraphrase Voltaire, it is our philosophy that although we may disapprove of what you write, we will defend to the death your right to write it."

Over the years, the awards have gone to a teacher who succeeded in restoring literary classics—including Steinbeck, Chaucer, and Aristophanes—that had been banned from Florida classrooms; an Arizona drama teacher who resisted censorship of a play selected for student production; a Denver bookstore owner who successfully challenged a Colorado law barring stores open to children from selling novels such as *For Whom the Bell Tolls* because of its alleged sexual content; a Missouri high school creative writing teacher who was fired for "failure to censor her students' creative expression"; a journalist who defeated a corporation's attempt to silence her written concerns about possible groundwater contamination caused by a local landfill; a

Maine writer harassed for her attempts to cover local industrial health hazards; a Florida high school teacher who struggled to defend literature in the classroom and press freedom for her students; the president of a Texas college who defended the production of Tony Kushner's play *Angels in America*; a high school librarian who fought to preserve access to library materials banned for sexual content (Steinbeck's *Of Mice and Men*, for instance); and last year's winner, a freelance writer who was jailed in a federal detention center in Texas for 128 days for refusing to bow to a sweeping subpoena of her confidential source materials.

CHAPTER 17

Dear Paul Newman:

In a world where they ram advertisements down our throats day after day, and in a world where the majority of those advertisements miss by a mile, here comes a product that makes us laugh when we read the label for one thing.

Then the next thing we notice is we don't get it crammed down our throat on TV and radio. Thank God!

My next thought was "another celebrity thinking we'll buy it because we like him as a star." Ha! I thought, not I!

But then recently instead of picking up my once every 3 months Ragú or whatever is on sale, I decided to give ole Paul Newman a break and picked up your Industrial Strength specialty. Being a gal who shrinks at all the preservatives, I did a double take at that label, Mr. Newman, and when I opened that jar I couldn't believe what I was seeing! What Ragú and some of the others say they have in their sauce (you have to carry a magnifying glass to see it) you put in yours! I've never seen real chunks of tomatoes, big slices of mushrooms and that taste! Wow! An honest man, I said to myself!

Thanks Paul Newman for putting a product on the market you must be very proud of. I sure feel good about buying it and feeding it to my husband. You've restored my faith in human nature. Yes, Helen, there is an honest manufacturer out there! Yahoo!

Respectfully,
Mrs. Helen Fox
Santa Cruz, CA

☞ We are sitting at our shared desk, the table from Paul's swimming pool patio, a large beach umbrella over our heads. There are two brass nameplates on the table, A. E. Hotchner, Lifeguard on Duty, and P. L. Newman, Assistant Lifeguard on Duty. It is two days before Christmas, and we are about to dispense all of this year's profits. We are still amazed that our little business lark has unbelievably turned us into philanthropists, a triumph of irresponsibility over reason.

In the beginning, we were bewildered, trying to decide which among the many deserving charities that had applied we should give to. But we eventually developed a reasonable concept—concentrating on organizations that were out of the mainstream of philanthropy. These profits give us a chance to repay those places that helped us when we needed them: Kenyon College, which whetted Paul's appetite for the stage; Yale University School of Drama, which firmed his resolve to be an actor; the Actors Studio in New York, where remarkable theater people taught and encouraged him and put both Joanne and him on the track to a career. Likewise, Hotch has been able to repay the St. Louis Scholarship Foundation and Washington University's Performing Arts School for what they contributed to his career. With our grants these schools can now help other young people as they helped us.

Of course, many of our donations go to major charities, such as Memorial Sloan-Kettering Cancer Center, Lahey Clinic, New York Foundling Hospital, Cystic Fibrosis Foundation, Society to Advance the Retarded and Handicapped, Harlem Restoration Project, and the American Foundation for AIDS Research. But the biggest kick we get is when we can help obscure little organizations that couldn't generate the publicity to attract the attention of donors.

For example, we received this letter written by Sister Carol Putnam, a Sacred Heart nun who runs the Hope Rural School in Indiantown, Florida: "I am hunting desperately for help for a new bus. Ours does not pass inspection for the fall. A new bus costs $26,000. I have written to several sources and have gotten a 'no' so far. A bus will last us ten years and we cannot pick up the children without one."

We phoned Sister Carol and discovered that Hope Rural, a school for the children of migrant farmworkers, might have to go out of existence because its fourteen-year-old secondhand school bus had been condemned.

Prior to the founding of the Hope Rural School, the children had been denied any consistent schooling. They were prevented from attending regular classes by the wretched poverty that forced their farmworker families to travel constantly throughout the country in search of seasonal work. The youngsters often labored in the fields alongside their parents, returning to central Florida every winter to harvest the state's citrus crops; when times got particularly hard, these families slept under bridges and in abandoned cars. Many of the children had never held a schoolbook or heard a nursery rhyme until the Hope Rural

School, built by the migrant workers themselves, began a flexible term that allowed the children to attend classes during the picking season without having to enroll in a normal September-to-June school year.

"But when our school bus was condemned this past summer by the state authorities, my worst fears were realized," Sister Carol told us. "With no bus to transport these children from their homes miles away, the school would be worthless, and many of the children would return to their hopeless lives in the fields."

Sister Carol said she had taken $1,000 that had been earmarked for teachers' salaries and put a down payment on a new school bus, hoping that somehow, some way, someone would donate money for the bus. The sisters at Hope Rural had written to foundations and called wealthy men and women from the nearby Palm Beach area, but the school could find no one willing to help. And then, the day before our phone call, as time and hope were running out, tragedy almost struck.

It was a blisteringly hot November afternoon, and the condemned school bus was making its way along back roads to bring a handful of students home for the day. As the bus approached the flashing lights of a railroad crossing, the driver applied the brakes, but the brakes wouldn't hold and the bus continued on toward the tracks. Warning whistles blared the approach of the Amtrak express from Tampa, but the driver decided to floor the gas pedal, charging across the tracks moments before the train swept by.

The very day that we spoke with Sister Carol, our check for the immediate delivery of a new bus to Hope Rural was on its way to the Blue Bird Bus Company.

In 1997, the nuns of Hope Rural informed us that the bus

had worn out after thirteen years of hard use, and we happily sent them a replacement.

☛ An intrepid editor cornered Paul one day and asked about his cooking credentials, seeing as how he was up to his whiskers in the food business. Paul gave her this straightforward answer:

"My adult life has been spent in the family of women: my wife, Joanne; five daughters; my housekeeper, Caroline; and a succession of wire-haired terriers, all males who were immediately castrated upon arrival. No wonder I took to wearing an apron by way of disguise, lest I become a capon. This apron which started out as a protective measure became, over time, an excuse to pursue the discovery of culinary treasures.

"The early discoveries resulted from my ability to establish a relationship with the food I'm about to cook. Have you ever had a meaningful conversation with a fillet of scrod? Or a dialogue with frog's legs?

"By way of preparation, I get ready by putting myself into a self-induced hypnotic trance, much in the same way the Shakirs trance themselves so that they can walk over hot coals and sleep comfortably on a bed of razor-sharp spikes.

"Once I'm in my trance, I hold the fillet of scrod in close proximity to my face, and pay attention. Sometimes I smell roses and think of flour. Sometimes I hear wedding bells, which translates to what? Mari-nade, of course. Church music and bedsprings? Then I cook like Joanne, who laughs like a whore and sings like an angel.

"You may be a bit skeptical of my method—as have been many before you—but to all those snicklers, snipers, and sniders I can only say that after the plates, knives, forks, napkins, and tablecloths are licked clean, nobody ever quarrels with the mystical, magical results of this intimate relationship between the chef and his victuals."

☛ Despite this, and other interviews like it, our sales continued to increase.

PART THREE

The Common Good

Give a little love to a child,

And get a great deal back.

—JOHN RUSKIN

I never thought I'd get into science,

but being able to turn salad dressing

into a school bus—that's the kind of

chemistry that tickles the fancy.

—P. LOQUESTO NEWMAN
TO JONAS SALK

CHAPTER

18

So one morning ol' PL woke up, December 1985, our fourth year of business, the day after the president and vice president had shoveled four million bucks into dozens of different charities: Memorial Sloan-Kettering, Cornell Medical, Flying Doctors, Meals-on-Wheels, Literacy Volunteers, a bunch. And if you haven't guessed it, yes! That's the morning ol' PL, in the privacy of his bathroom, had thumped his chest mightily and often, strutted about, gloating that this idiot company had not only survived but had given back more than anyone had ever hoped or expected. It was later learned that Hotch also, in the privacy of *his* bathroom, had grinned at his image in the mirror, muttering, "Hot diggety, hot diggety."

And yet . . .

And yet something was missing, something that everyone in the company needed, not knowing they needed but needed anyway, something that ol' PL and Hotch could have as their very own—a project that could be dear to their hearts, a project that PL says he just "woke up with," a project that happened to be a camp for children with life-threatening diseases, the circumstances, he says, best explained in a foreword he later wrote for a book written about the camp, which he had christened the Hole in the Wall Gang—the name taken from the legendary hideout of Butch Cassidy and the Sundance Kid:

> I wish I could recall with clarity the impulse that compelled me to help bring this camp into being. I'd be pleased if I could announce a motive of lofty purpose. I've been accused of compassion, of altruism, of devotion to Christian, Hebrew, and Moslem ethic, but however desperate I am to claim ownership of a high ideal, I cannot.
>
> I wanted, I think, to acknowledge Luck: the chance of it, the benevolence of it in my life, and the brutality of it in the lives of others: made especially savage for children because they may not be allowed the good fortune of a lifetime to correct it.

We had already visited children at risk. One of the charities we supported was the New York Foundling Hospital, where many of those deserted children were physically impaired. We also supported the Children's Burn Unit at the Cornell Medical Center, run by a remarkably caring physician, Dr. Willibald Nagler. We had visited children there who were recovering from catastrophic burns that threatened their lives. We certainly had sympathy for these embattled children, but if we were to give them an uplifting experience, we needed to inform ourselves as to what kind of facility would be ideal for the incipient Hole in the Wall Gang Camp. We visited Hemlocks, a Connecticut facility for the handicapped that didn't operate in the summer. It was an institutionalized structure, unadorned, a severe concoction of glass and steel. We could have operated our camp there during the summer months, but walking through those antiseptic buildings, we realized that our camp should not look like that.

We flew out to California to visit a camp called Camp Good Times, which operated for several weeks for children with cancer. It was run by a woman named Pepper Abrams, who was very informative about the children and their illnesses, about the camp programs, and about the support staff that was needed. She also introduced us to the camp doctor, Dr. Stuart Siegel, and gave us insight into the medical aspect of their operation. But Good Times did not have its own campsite—it rented space from an existing camp.

We visited a camp in Blairstown, New Jersey, Memorial Sloan-Kettering's Happiness Is Camping. The doctor in charge was a pediatric oncologist, Dr. Paul Meyers, a very knowledgeable, engaging man who educated us on the special camping needs of children with cancer. Happiness Is Camping was a successful endeavor, but it was not built for the special needs of this population of children, and Dr. Meyers agreed that a specific camp such as the one we envisioned would be infinitely better.

We felt that the time had come for us to find a site where we could build the Hole in the Wall. To help us in this search, we enlisted the assistance of Marc Nevas, the son of our lawyer, who ran a local real estate firm. The first site he found was north of New Haven, attractive land that had the drawback of being adjacent to a power line; we were advised that these power lines could possibly disseminate fields of energy that would be detrimental to the health of the campers. Marc showed us good acreage with a lake in Old Lyme, Connecticut, but its reputation as the original source of Lyme ticks discouraged us. We also looked at a facility in Torrington, Connecticut, owned by the YMCA that had once been a Boy Scout camp but had deteriorated and was now up for sale. The buildings were rickety, and it had a lodge that was in precarious shape; what's more, the rotting dock was about to fall into the lake. But Paul, who was very anxious to go forward, enthusiastically embraced an immediate plan to fix up the lodge, the cabins, and the dock. A contract had not been executed for the acquisition of this site, but Paul had confidence that the deal would go through, and work was immediately started on the lodge. A state-of-the-art kitchen was installed, the fireplace was reconstructed, and some serious money was expended.

It was at this point that the YMCA people informed us that with the money they would receive from us for the purchase of this property, they would establish a camp for the Boy Scouts on the other side of the lake and share facilities with our camp. Although well-meaning, that was certainly not what we had in mind, sick children with cancer having to share a location with healthy, robust ones. Paul was about to take off for Chicago to make *The Color of Money* with Tom Cruise, but before leaving, he agreed with Hotch that we should add up our losses and remove ourselves from this situation, which we did, leaving behind a refurbished lodge and a new dock.

The Torrington episode did nothing to dampen Paul's enthusiasm. When he's on location, in between takes, Paul has time on his hands, so during this shoot he was often on the phone with Hotch discussing the camp, which he now envisioned as a camp that would look not like a camp, but like a little town where Butch Cassidy might have hung out.

Marc Nevas was proposing other places to be inspected when Paul returned, but it occurred to us that we were going about this ass-backward. We realized that Pepper Abrams's reliance on Dr. Siegel, who she had said was the "heart and soul of my camp," and Dr. Paul Meyers, who was so vital to Happiness Is Camping, indicated that we would be better off starting with a doctor and then, with his medical input, exploring a campsite. Hotch made an appointment with a Dr. Howard Pearson, who was chairman of the Department of Pediatrics at Yale–New Haven Hospital and the senior pediatric blood doctor in Connecticut.

Dr. Pearson is a soft-spoken, attentive man with a wicked sense of humor and a tenderness about him that comes from long years of treating sick children. When he heard what we wanted to do, he leaned across the desk and said, "What do you need?" We didn't know that, providentially, Dr. Pearson was just completing a fourteen-year term as chairman of the Department of Pediatrics at Yale and that he imminently would have free time to devote to our undertaking.

In addition to becoming our camp doctor, Doc Pearson brought two other very important Yale people into our circle: Vince Conti, who was vice president of administration for Yale–New Haven, and Tom Beeby, who was dean of the School of Architecture. Vince is a warm, compassionate, caring, very intelligent man whose structured thinking and sense of organization would become vital to the diffuse beginning of the camp. And, as it turned out, Dean Beeby brought an inspired concept to the design and building of the camp.

☞ But long after Paul had finished *The Color of Money*, we were still searching for that elusive campsite, and when we did find it, we almost let it slip away. Again, the location originated with Marc Nevas, but he was not sanguine about its potential because he considered it too close to an adjacent roadway. Nonetheless, Ursula Gwynne decided to take time off from her office duties and visit the property, which was located in the little town of Ashford, Connecticut, near the Massachusetts border, about equidistant from all the major population centers in the Northeast. Ursula took one look at it and immediately alerted us to its possibilities. What we found were three hundred pristine, mostly level acres with a forty-five-acre pond, completely undeveloped, covered with exquisite wildflowers and frondescence.

It was also covered with swarms of pesky mayflies, mosquitoes, and other such attackers that we had to fight off. The next time we visited the location, Paul was prepared for the swarming onslaught—he wore a chef's hat that had an indented peak in which he had put a large glob of strawberry jam, so while everyone else was battling the flying critters, Paul's attackers were buzzing all around his hat but leaving him alone.

Contrary to Marc's observation, we felt the property was far enough removed from highways that we would not have to be concerned about security. We realized that this site would require everything—electric and phone lines, septic tanks, roadways, fences, walkways, abridgments, landscaping, various permits, and every other amenity you could think of—but we immediately went about the business of acquiring the land from the Harakaly family, who had owned it for many years. George Harakaly became our maintenance director, and during the camp's formative years, he was an integral part of its physical development. Getting title to the land was easy compared to the effort it took to get approval from the towns of Ashford and Eastford (a small part of the land was in Eastford). To that end, Paul sent this persuasive letter to Rudolph Makray, who was chairman of the Ashford Planning and Zoning Commission:

> The general concept for this camp arose as the result of the demand and need that I became aware of in the last two years. The requests for funds for the benefit of youngsters who are critically, and in many cases terminally, ill call me to embark on this project. It is my hope that this project will bring some peace and happiness to some suffering children and some respite from their pain and anguish. I am certain that the town of Ashford and the entire area will have good reason to be proud of this project, and the important role that this camp will have in the lives of many children of this area. I think that the camp in Ashford will become known for this humanitarian project in which all of us are engaged.
>
> As I approach my dotage, I become acutely aware of the privilege of long life and the sense of accomplishment and completion that can be run from that simple piece of good fortune. At the same time it reminds me that some children, at a whim and perverse stroke of bad fortune, are deprived of that privilege.
>
> It occurred to me how rewarding it might be for us of privilege if we were able to provide some few weeks for these young people where they could be together, establish common bonds under the umbrella of an old-fashioned camp experience—the likes of which I remember so vividly from my childhood.

☛ In addition to the zoning commission, there were many meetings with a committee of townspeople (one of these meetings attended by the governor of Connecticut) and endless meetings with various local functionaries to acquire the many permits required for septic tanks, power lines, camping, and so forth.

At this time we received a letter from a Dr. Sam Ross, who operated Green Chimneys, a nearby camp for disturbed children, offering his expertise however we might be able to use it. Dr. Ross wrote:

> I built and have operated the Green Chimneys School and Children's Services since 1947. It operates 365 days a year and I've been here since its inception. After graduating from Stanford Medical School, my son who had Hodgkin's Disease realized that he could not pursue the profession of doctoring because the disease had become too debilitating. I had recently seen a small article in Fundraising Magazine that Paul Newman and A. E. Hotchner were going to open a camp for children with terminal illness. My son David and I both saw the article and David said why don't you contact them, Dad, you know how to run camps. Perhaps you can be of help. I'm sure that the people at Yale–New Haven Hospital will provide you with splendid medical participation, but I can offer you my expertise in the educational, recreational, vocational, and psychological programs that you may find necessary.

☛ We immediately took up Dr. Ross on his offer and found that we had acquired a truly unique man, wise, outgoing, perceptive, a vital contributor to the camp's beginning and, over the years, to its enduring quality.

So now we had the land and the team to organize the camp, but to everyone's astonishment, we also had an impossibly impatient P. L. Newman, who was obsessed with getting it all done, from architectural plans to finished campsite, within a year.

Everyone said it couldn't be done.

Paul's attitude was: What we did with our salad dressing, we will now do for this camp.

Five summers ago I came to the Hole in the Wall for the first time. I was a short-haired twelve-year-old suffering from non-Hodgkins lymphoma and undergoing chemotherapy. It wasn't until my second year that I realized the friends I made here were unlike my friends anywhere else. I had the best summer of my life—until the next summer came, and that was the best. And the next—and that was the best. So it has been for the past five summers. But now I am well and this was my last summer and my best summer in this place that has become such a stronghold in my life. This isn't a camp <u>about</u> sick children. <u>For</u> sick children, yes. But once you drive through those gates, that's not what it's about at all. It's about life. A life that all of the campers never got to lead anywhere else, and hopefully most of the children of the world will never have to face. This camp is a nest where I hatched my personality and my life. I love this place and the people that represent it, and from this point on, no matter where I go or what I do, the Hole in the Wall will be there with me.

—NORAH MORRIS

CHAPTER

19

When Dean Beeby heard that we intended to have the camp up and running in a year's time, he did everything he could to talk us out of it. "It is now June 1987," Dean Beeby said. "Do you think we can throw this thing together and have this whole business built and running by June 1988? Let me read this list of things that will have to be done: septic tanks, freshwater wells, roads, telephone and electric lines, Olympic-size state-of-the-art heated swimming pool, twenty-two buildings, some of them, like the dining building, very complicated, thirteen log cabins made from special Canadian logs, the lake dredged, interiors finished, electronics, infirmary totally outfitted with all its complicated medical paraphernalia ... We don't even have the architectural plans yet; normally it takes a year just to go from sketches to finished plans. All the permits that you will need from health inspectors, fire, sanitary, wetlands, telephone grids, electrical plans, golf carts, trucks, office equipment, garden stuff, mowers, all that, computers—and what about finances? You're budgeted at ten million, which you'll have to raise. And then there's staffing—counselors, maintenance, kitchen, cooks, and also insurance. You'll be lucky to open in 1989."

We stuck to our guns. We would be open in a year's time. We had sloughed off the discouragement and pessimism of the marketing and production experts who told us what we had to do and the big bucks it would cost, and once again we would defy the experts.

They said, "What if you do succeed in lining up a bunch of sick kids for next summer, and then have to disappoint them because you're not ready?"

"But if we are ready," we said, "then one thousand sick kids will have a summer that they wouldn't have otherwise. That's the risk—if we make it, they make it."

"There's no way that we can begin building until fall," the architects said, "which means construction all through the winter. You know how tough a winter up there can be. Blizzards and ice and the thermometer way down there."

"We're a couple of gamblers on a roll," we said. "It's not the first time we've bet against the house."

We had learned from Doc Pearson that cancer is the most prevalent childhood disease everywhere in the world. We could bring kids to the camp from all over this country, everywhere. Doc said that 70 percent of the children did not make it, but 30 percent survived—in either case, we knew that if we got it right, we'd give them a hell of a good time, away from the hospitals. If we got this right, we'd be able to open other camps, be the trigger; so the sooner we opened up, the better. Doc said that some of these kids hadn't had any experience outside their homes and hospitals. Those camps we had seen, how institutional they were. If we got it right, our camp would be as institutional as a gypsy.

☞ "The first time I met with Paul and Hotch," Tom Beeby says, "it was at the Newman's Own office, the office furnished with Paul's old lawn furniture, and a Ping-Pong table with personalized paddles. Hilarious signs on the walls. It was great stuff. Once I saw that, the notion of what might be possible dawned on me, that this was not an ordinary client. These were a couple of guys who were willing to take risks, had a great sense of humor, and were willing to try anything. So that opened up the idea that we could do something really special. Before that, I had the expectation of a normal job. But once I realized how free they were of ordinary conventions, then I realized we could expand what we might be able to do there.

"From the very beginning, Paul wanted to create a semblance of the western town of *Butch Cassidy and the Sundance Kid*. So I was trying to sort through that as an architectural idea, which seemed like a curious concept for a Connecticut site. In addition to my position at Yale, I have an architectural firm in Chicago, and I was working on this with some of my key people."

Beeby's initial scheme was like a traditional camp, with a main building in the town center. Our reaction wasn't good. We told him it was too institutional. Paul made it clear that we wanted something that was extremely unarchitectural, something capricious and freewheeling and not in any way orthodox or doctrinaire. So the architects went back to their drawing boards to create a town, with the town center where the major buildings were, with the cabins as a kind of settlement around it. The dining hall would look like a public gathering space but have an overlay of being a Shaker barn. The administration building looked like the town hall, it had columns and a pediment, and it was a classical temple, so it would be the center of power, with stores running down the street. And each one had a symbolic sign that signified what craft went on inside. The gym became the livery stable with bark columns on it.

"Paul's architectural theory," Beeby says, "was that whenever you got to the point where you'd make something more the same or more different, always make it more different. Both of them were against any kind of regimentation or anything that had to do with institutionalization. So we created this overtone of a very lighthearted, fun place, with a kind of dream world aspect to it. This town was a fantasy place where kids would go and forget their past, forget their current medical problems. That evolved as the major theme of the camp, and the look was rather cinematic. Everyone was very candid. They said what they thought. Paul and Hotch would balance these things and in the end make a decision on it. So it moved very rapidly. It was not a normal building process where you mulled over these things forever, because there was no structure at that point to the camp. Paul and Hotch decided things right on the spot. There was a lot of brainstorming, and a lot of crazy ideas were thrown out. Paul and Hotch worked as a team. Paul was obviously the inspirational driving force behind it. Hotch was always there as a kind of foil to Paul. He would always have an opinion, sometimes different, sometimes the same. They had great rapport. They bantered about things in a way that was quite amusing but very effective. Hotch had a lot of ideas, some workable, some not. But Paul always kept a firm hand on the tiller."

Beeby brought in people from his Chicago office, and they did all the architectural drawing on the dining room table of the local motel where they were staying. They did freehand drawings, which they presented to us; we would make suggestions, they would revise the sketches and then bring them back to

Chicago. All the buildings were different. So everybody in Beeby's office got one building to design, more than thirty buildings. They had three days to design a building, and then they would hang up all the drawings on the wall in the office and everybody would cross-critique one another's buildings. But the personality of each person's building was carefully maintained. They didn't homogenize the buildings in any way—thus the buildings were quite different because different people did them, and that gave the whole camp a diversity and life that it wouldn't have had otherwise.

To avoid the institutionalized furniture of ordinary camps, three of Beeby's employees went to flea markets all over the Midwest and bought truckloads of furniture.

"At a certain point, I began to get nervous about what we had bought," Beeby says, "because a lot of it was rickety and very strange looking. I wasn't sure that Hotch and Paul would go for it. So I asked them to come to Chicago and take a look at this huge stockpile of furnishings. They did, and their enthusiasm for it matched mine. It was a perfect strategy for this camp, because with this kind of lunatic inventory you can endlessly replace individual pieces and not have to worry about systems of furniture and all that kind of stuff. We had to go directly into production from the drawings. Each building had its own cycle, and we finished them as fast as we could. We did those working drawings in a matter of weeks, turned them over as fast as we could. It wasn't easy because they ended up being complicated buildings. It was all heavy timber. On one occasion the timbers for the dining hall were lost. The train had left Montana, but it never got to Connecticut. We traced it and finally found it somewhere on a siding in northern Minnesota.

"And then there were the difficulties with the log cabins. We went to Canada to see a man who was an expert on making log cabins. We ended up in the middle of nowhere, a remote shack with workers in the yard behind it, peeling logs and making these log cabins. There was a kind of archaic Stone Age aspect to the whole thing. Making log cabins is difficult, because when you have green timber it shrinks eight or ten inches. So we had to design all the windows to provide for shrinkage of the logs. Nobody in the States is familiar with that process, but these Canadian guys were very smart and figured out how to do it.

"We'd never done anything this ad hoc or this fast. We used to meet in restaurants, and during dinner we'd roll out the drawings on the floor in the middle of the restaurant while people were dining, and we talked through the buildings while eating dinner at the same time. We worked through the buildings sequentially and eventually got approval on all of them. Paul had a lot of faith in everybody. He just assumed it was going to turn out all right. He never questioned the ability of anybody. He never suggested that it was a hard task. He just wanted to have it done, and he wasn't unreasonable, but he was totally involved during the design phase. He knew every finish, the hardware, every detail went by him.

"Building this camp was unique in that all the bureaucracy that usually surrounds building construction was absent. There was a kind of magic about the construction from the very beginning, because everyone was there because they were dedicated to doing it. And everybody believed in the cause. The construction process is normally kind of antagonistic. The different people that make up the team usually are at odds with one another—the contractor, the architect, the owner—but in this case, we transcended all the usual building problems, and the spirit of the place transferred onto the building process. We were like little kids building sand castles. It had an unreal aspect to it. That's why I think it has such an amazing aura to it. It has this kind of sheer, pure imagination applied to the building process, to the way the land is used, the way the buildings were conceived. I think everyone imagined what it would be like to have kids use these buildings and how they'd move from building to building. And all that was really built into it from the very beginning. I've never been involved with a project like this. It was a magic moment."

No matter what the difficulties were, we pushed through them. For instance, the problem with the lake. We were going to build a beach where the kids could swim. The U.S. Army Corps of Engineers volunteered to do it. They mucked the bottom and reinforced the dam. But when they got to where the beach was supposed to be and started to dredge that out, they found an enormous number of water snakes in there. Huge water snakes. So everyone lost their enthusiasm for having the beach there.

There were meetings to win various permissions from local officials, but initially we didn't do very well. The first time, it was the architects and the people from Yale meeting local officials in the back room of the library. The locals were very bureaucratic. Small New England towns run things their own way. So they set up a lot of roadblocks, and it appeared that they weren't going to be too helpful. So Beeby asked Paul to attend the next meeting. A month later when we went up to Ashford, the meeting had moved from the back room of the library to the school gymnasium, and there were four hundred people there instead of four. As for the permissions we had requested, whatever Paul wanted was fine with them.

"During the actual building," Beeby says, "there was always this kind of play between the serious and the funny, something that Hotch and Paul were both very good at. They had an ironic sense of what was amusing, with an overlay of seriousness. And that's really what the camp was all about. When you talk to Paul and Hotch, there's this sense that life is really serious, but you can't take it too seriously. And out of humor and amusing situations, profound ideas can be communicated. I think that in the end, that fed its way into the camp. I think that when you go there, you have the sense that it's a fun place, that it's amusing, but not in a Disney-like sense. And there's obviously a kind of tragic aspect to the camp because of the nature of the kids that are there. And they actually work together in a way that I think is quite profound."

Camp is a place where you learn to live life better because you can do all sorts of things you thought you'd never do again, like fishing or horseback riding, because it's hard getting on a horse even without having had a stroke. Camp teaches you that you can do other things than lie in a hospital bed or lie in a grave forever. I think it's real cool that it doesn't cost anything because the kids don't have much money left because they paid all the hospital bills. And it's great that they can finally go have fun. And live while they can. I met new people, and it's so good to meet other sick kids because they can help you through when you're having trouble, and you help them when they're down. Like I helped David. He was really crying 'cause he had cancer in his brain, and I talked to him and I cheered him up. He was so cute, I just couldn't resist. I told him my story, that I had a brain tumor and I got radiation and now it's all gone. It made him feel better because I gave him hope that you've got a good friend. And maybe when you're down, he'll cheer you up. I don't care if my boyfriend has no hair because I was like that, too. I'm not afraid to see it. I think that hope and love and laughing and confidence are all over camp; in a way they're growing as much as the grass is.

—KATIE MARTIN

I have been meaning to write this letter for some time now. When our daughter Breezy was diagnosed with AML (Acute Myelogenous Leukemia) one week after her eighth birthday last March, our entire family was completely blindsided. Breezy had always been a perfectly healthy, active, and beautiful young girl. She went to school, enjoyed her friends, and *quarreled with her brother and sister just like any other normal eight-year-old would. She had never been sick, and never needed any hospital stays or treatments for any specific disorders or diseases. She was very likeable, and easy to get along with and the apple of her Dad's eye. Her dirty blonde hair was shoulder length, and she was fair-skinned with dimples when she smiled, which she did quite often. Needless to say, we were shattered when we discovered how very sick she had become, and now there was talk of chemotherapy, transfusions, and possible bone marrow transplantation. Chemo was successful in arresting the disease for several months, during which Breezy was able to attend The Hole in the Wall Gang Camp in August 1997. Leaving her there was one of the most difficult acts I can remember.*

Suddenly, The Hole in the Wall Gang Camp became her camp. She showed us all her crafts and doodads she had made, told us stories of riding the horses and of swimming. Breezy was later invited back to participate in the Gala in September. She had such a good time meeting Julia Roberts, Paul Newman, Carole King and many others, and we were honored to see her up on stage and then later to see the video copy that was sent to us. We will treasure it forever. Breezy was also able to attend the reunion in November, as well as the Christmas party in December. In fact, one of the best family pictures we treasure at home is one of Mr. and Mrs. Claus sitting with all four of our children on their laps! Breezy looked so very happy and healthy in that picture, little were we to know that she was to become so very sick within a couple of weeks and that she would die in February of this year.

We thank all of you at the Camp for making her last sum-

mer here on Earth a little brighter. Recently I found a copy of her camp song book and noticed that one page was dog-eared at her favorite song which she loved to sing—"Stars in the Sky."

—SUE ĐIĐOMIZIO

CHAPTER 20

The goddess of luck certainly gave us a thumbs-up that fall. To begin with, a wonderful man named Simon Konover, who had come to the United States as an impecunious Russian immigrant and started what became one of the biggest construction companies in Connecticut, offered to supervise construction without a fee, normally 10 percent of the total cost. He then furnished the man who would be the most important person to the entire operation—the construction supervisor. When he first appeared, an affable twenty-six-year-old with little experience, Newman went nuts. He called Konover. "Simon, you sent us a kid in diapers! A cream-puff. We're sunk."

"Just wait," Simon said, and hung up.

Mike Kolakowski proved he was no kid in diapers. He was a cross between Dale Carnegie and John Bunyan. He had the mind-set of a bulldog and the endurance of a panhandler working 42nd Street. He set himself up in a trailer on the site and operated out of it like an army command general in the field. He figured out how to build sequentially in a way that didn't make sense on paper, but it made sense the way he built it, finishing buildings as he went, one after the other. He'd wrap each one in

Visqueen, milky plastic sheets, to keep it from getting muddy, and then he'd move on to the next building. He was very resourceful, and he kept everybody in a positive frame of mind. Newman began to call him "the Ax."

When fall turned to winter, Lady Luck turned out to be not much of a lady. It was one of the coldest winters on record—record snowfall, sustained subfreezing temperatures, ice storms, high-velocity winds, arctic conditions.

The Ax was unperturbed. He had few takers for the jobs at hand and finally had to resort to hunting in Canada to find workers who were used to frigid winter conditions. No matter how low the thermometer went or how dense the blizzard, these men constructed the cabins, which had a difficult tongue-and-groove assembly that eschewed nails. We drove up to the camp one day through the snow and ice and hosted dinner for the men at the Rusty Nail, a smoky tavern near the site that had pool tables, draft beer, and lumberjack food. Fast Eddie played pool with the guys and lost (purposely?), tossed darts, spoon-fed them Budweiser. He joined the workers as both cheerleader and coach, telling his merciless jokes, posing for Instamatics, autographing shirts, menus, and even the top of a bald pate or two. They were a dedicated, gung ho team, ready to rush out for the Gipper through snowbanks and howling wind and score the winning touchdown in the final minutes.

☛ Dr. Pearson says, "My priority was to equip and staff a complete medical facility and then to find a way to induce sick children to come to the camp. I convened a meeting in Newman's barn in Westport (in the stable area below us was where the Newman's Own Salad Dressing had been born) with all the directors of hematology/oncology in New England: Boston's Children's Hospital, Dana-Farber, Mass General, Tufts, Worcester, Springfield, New Haven, Hartford. It was a medical think tank with a unique mission—no one had ever built a camp that was physically and programmatically tailor-made from the ground up for the special needs of these children. We tried to figure out how many of these sick children might be available to go to camp. How we would be able to convince parents and physicians that we could anticipate emergencies and handle them if they arose.

"Our highest priority was to take children who, because of their diseases or because of their complications or because of their treatment, couldn't go to an ordinary camp. They'd primarily come to the camp to have fun and get away from the grim medical routines of their lives, but they would not come to the camp for treatment—they might *need* treatment to be at camp, but that would be secondary. Our infirmary would contain emergency equipment to rival that of any hospital, and we would put into place protocols to cover almost every conceivable complication. We would also have a landing pad for a helicopter so that in a severe life-threatening emergency we could airlift the child to the Yale–New Haven Hospital, which by air was only thirty minutes away. We would have doctors and a staff of nurses on duty around the clock, so that we would be able to perform procedures not available at ordinary camps. We would be able to give blood transfusions, platelet transfusions, and intravenous chemotherapy, which would enable us to take really sick children."

☞ As soon as the winter relented, we were overwhelmed by a giving phenomenon that continues to this day—an outpouring of spontaneous unsolicited contributions: a local well digger donated four wells; 250 mattresses were contributed by a Hartford mattress company; members of the Connecticut State Legislature hosted a ball at which Hotch was presented with a check sufficient to build the boathouse; Paul flew to St. Louis to see Augustus Busch (Budweiser sponsored Paul's race car) and walked away from the meeting with a check that covered the cost, nearly $1 million, of building the centerpiece of the camp, the dining hall; the Eastern Airlines Silverliners (retired flight attendants) raised $11,000; the U.S. Army Corps of Engineers dredged the entire lake and repaired the dam; the U.S. Navy Seabees built a network of bridges across wetlands and marsh areas that entirely circumnavigated the camp; members of the Connecticut Swimming Pool Association, usually fierce competitors, banded together to donate the swimming pool: one company dug the hole, another gunited it, another did the tiling, another installed the heating equipment, another built the bathhouses—an amazing feat of cooperation that resulted in a state-of-the-art Olympic-size swimming pool that would have cost approximately $1 million. On its completion, all the members of the association held a baptism party at the pool, which was blessed by a consortium of clerics, a priest, a rabbi, and a minister. It was a joyous occasion, this magnificent pool created by a banding of competitors who, on that day, glorified charity. The next day, as usual, they all went for one another's throat in happy competition.

All through that spring we were flooded with contributions from firefighters, hairdressing salons, community groups, and school groups who staged walk-a-thons, talk-a-thons, jump-a-thons, bike-a-thons, every conceivable "thon" with the exception of study-a-thons. An eight-year-old boy sent in $5.40, which he had earned from operating a lemonade stand the previous summer.

A local woman, Charlotte Werner, who would eventually become food service and dining hall manager, donated food and drink when needed and started gardens in an effort to overcome the bare, muddy patches left in the wake of the bulldozers.

☞ As important as these donations were, it was equally important to receive financial contributions. According to IRS regulations, Newman's Own could provide only 50 percent of the cost of building the camp; the rest had to be obtained from other corporate and individual sources. One of those who early on volunteered to help with fund-raising was Ray LaMontagne, an investment banker who also over the years became a valued member of the board of directors, eventually taking over the chairmanship.

One day Paul received a call about a young man from Saudi Arabia, Khaled Alhegelan, who lived in Washington, D.C., and wanted to come see him at our Connecticut office. He was afflicted with a rare blood disease, one that required all his blood to be transfused regularly, and he wanted to know about this incipient camp he had heard about. He came up on the train, a bright, very pleasant young man. He and Paul played Ping-Pong and discussed the model of the camp that was mounted beside the Ping-Pong table. What a boon, Khaled said, such a camp would have been to him as a sickly, isolated child if one had existed. He said he would like to help with funding for the camp.

Paul said, "Yup," which, translated, means, "I hear you, but I don't expect much."

Twelve days later, Khaled phoned to say that King Fahd had made a donation, but that to receive it we would have to attend a presentation ceremony at the Saudi embassy in D.C. A group of us went as a delegation, totally unprepared for the check they handed Paul for the Hole in the Wall Gang—$5 million! Since Saudi custom permits any citizen to petition the king for an audience, Khaled requested a donation. Khaled's father had been ambassador to Venezuela and Washington, which gave him an edge, to say the least. The camp was now practically paid for, although subsequent construction—like the theater that we built two years later—escalated the final costs considerably. Khaled has been a valuable member of the camp's board of directors since its inception.

☞ Despite blizzards, pervading skepticism, and balky permits, we had gone full speed ahead, hiring a camp director (through a search committee); recruiting counselors from universities; staffing the kitchen; arranging for horses; equipping the boathouse with rowboats, canoes, and fishing tackle; outfitting the arts and crafts buildings, the office, the gymnasium, the children's cabins, and the library; and installing furry and feathered residents in the petting zoo.

The last workmen, the bulldozers, and the construction trailers pulled out virtually as the first children began to arrive in June 1988. And there we were that first day, standing in the reception area, waiting for our first 100 kids to arrive. Imagine our disappointment when only 46 showed up. Paul's name being attached to the camp didn't cut much mustard with the parents of sick kids. We thought we had been born with credentials— we weren't. That first session, we had more counselors than campers; it turned out to be a blessing that we were only half-full. With a full complement of children, our inexperienced staff would have been completely overwhelmed. But half-filled, we had time for a shakedown and were able to work out a lot of the wrinkles.

☛ "We were all first-time counselors in a first-time camp," says Jimmy Canton, now executive director. "We had a week of orientation before the first batch of kids were to arrive. Every night we would gather together in the dining hall, the entire staff in a circle. There were about forty or fifty of us, and we asked questions: How are we going to run our programs? What is the schedule going to be? What do we do after meals? That first session we had more staff than we had kids, and we were asking kids to please stay, session after session, so that we would have the beds filled.

"I can clearly recall the last night of that first session of kids. [Each session lasted eight to nine days.] We were out behind the yellow unit cabins, singing a song: 'We're all together again right here, right here. / We're all together again right here, right here. / And I don't know when we'll be together again, / But we're all together again right here, right here.' I was holding the hand of this little boy, named Wilson, who was a really hard kid. I had not been able to get through at all to him, all session. He had been reluctant to put his guard down. Holding his hand as we're singing that song, I thought to myself, It's raining out. And I remember looking up and thinking, There's no rain around here. He was crying right onto my hand.

"After the song, we went back into the cabin and said good night to the kids, who were now weeping, uncontrollably weeping. I got so upset myself that I walked outside to where there was a big rock outside the yellow unit and climbed up on the rock. And I could hear them crying in the camper bedroom. They were eight-, nine-year-old boys. And I just sat on the rock and I too started to cry and I began to pray, asking God to help me get through the summer because at that moment, I didn't know if I could make it.

"Another thing happened right after that first session: One of our campers died a few days after he left camp. That rocked all of us. The counselors realized that they needed some kind of processing moment, a cleansing, a time to recollect. So we went down to where there was a little tepee beside the lake, and we built a campfire. There was a big log there, and we lit candles all along it. The boy's name was Philip. We shared stories about him, what we remembered about the session, how grateful we were that we had the time with him. He was a really sick boy, but it never occurred to us that he would not make it.

"When kids come to camp you can see the frailty in them physically. You haven't gotten to know them well enough to determine if it is emotional. It wasn't like, Oh, this poor kid. Or, Oh, this is too much. It was, He needs attention. He needs love. Let's make this really special. And that's not something you can teach. I think that the counselors who came here knew that this was a beautiful opportunity to share this time with that boy."

☛ We anticipated that the atmosphere of this camp for kids with cancer, 70 percent of whom would eventually die, would have a hospital aura. Kids who were being treated for leukemia, who were undergoing radiation, chemotherapy, and other forms of medication that would be debilitating. Many would have lost their hair, some of them had lost limbs, some had open catheters in their chests. The great shock was that this was not at all a somber, hospital-type experience, but a joyful one for the children and for us. These children had the time of their lives from the moment they set foot on the campgrounds, whether they were in a wheelchair, on crutches, whatever, the ones that could walk pushed the ones who couldn't. The ones who had hair painted the bald heads of the ones who had no hair. It was a release for all of them.

They'd been pent-up in hospitals, living in communities where they were outcasts and other kids made fun of them. They couldn't play sports. They were denied so many things. Now suddenly the camp put them in an environment with kids who were in the same boat they were in. And they were being told, Yes, get up on this horse, you can ride a horse. We may have to hold you, walk with you, but you will ride a horse. Come out on the boat. You can catch a fish. This was all new to them. They were having the most fun of their young lives.

We don't know what motivated that first group of young counselors, most of them college students. They arrived with a fierce enthusiasm and a spirit that to us the Hole in the Wall Gang epitomized. It exists today; it's been that way ever since the camp opened. When visitors come and they observe the attitude of the children and these counselors, they ask, What does this come from? It's almost as if there's special water you drink there. But the big surprise was that this was such an uplifting experience, for the children and for anybody around them, including us.

From the beginning we thought of this as a year-round facility, not for camping necessarily, but we thought that in the off-season it could be used as a retreat for parents who had lost children, who could interact about their mutual experiences, their feelings. For siblings who had lost brothers and sisters. For nurses who needed to have a weekend away from exhausting chores. For oncology doctors when they wanted to have a convention of ideas there. Many different ways that the camp could be used in the off-season. We have sporadically sponsored some of these activities, but now that we are building a new lodge, we intend to have full winter programs.

Doc Pearson says, "I've worked with children with sickle-cell disease, a genetic blood disorder, all my doctoring life. There are literally thousands of these afflicted kids, primarily African American, whose lives will be shortened by the disease. It gets its name from the shape of the red blood cells, which are sickle shaped with pointed ends instead of round, which is the normal shape, enabling the blood cells to roll smoothly through the veins. But sickle cells are prone to embed their pointed ends in the walls of the veins, causing intense, unbearable pain, a crisis that often requires morphine and other strong pain suppressors.

"These children, subject to these violent, devastating attacks, are not accepted by ordinary camps, but we set up special sessions for them. We learned that one thing that set off these crises was going into a swimming pool that had ordinary temperature. And so we hit on the idea of jacking up the temperature of the pool to an unheard-of eighty-five to ninety degrees during the sickle-cell sessions. The result was that for many of them, it's the first time they can really swim—in fact, the first time they can even enter a swimming pool. How gratifying it is to look at the pool during the sickle-cell sessions and see wall-to-wall kids enjoying swimming for the first time in their lives.

To protect them when they come out, we built a gazebo with heaters in the surface that counselors called the french fryer. So they come out of the pool and dry off and get warm, and the painful episodes associated with swimming and sickle-cell disease have virtually vanished."

☛ Back in 1990, when HIV was still an unexplained mystery and of great concern to the population at large, there was a kind of hysteria about it. Children were being prevented from going to school because of HIV. Families were being chased out of town because their kids had HIV. There was, of course, no possible opportunity for these children to have a summer camping experience, so when Doc Pearson came to us with the suggestion that we set up an early pilot session for children who had vertically transmitted HIV—that is, HIV acquired from their mothers at birth—we informed ourselves as much as possible about the risks that might be involved. As a result of the research we did, it was our conviction that there was no real significant risk of casual exposure. We decided to go ahead with an experimental session, which we called an "immunology session," thereby glossing over the HIV label. Families were very concerned that their children might be stigmatized by attending such a session, so we imposed strict rules that they couldn't be photographed, nor could the children be identified by name. It turned out to be a felicitous move, for as the years passed and general expert information was disseminated about HIV, there was an acceptance of what we had recognized in the beginning, that there was no reason not to provide these children with a camping experience.

My name is Kelsey Taylor. I'm eight years old and I have Sickle Cell Anemia. I've had Sickle Cell all my life.

Sickle Cell causes my cells to be different from everyone else's cells, because my cells are shaped like hard bananas and they get stuck in my veins and I have pain. Also, every time I have a temperature of 101 degrees I have to go to the hospital and get IV fluids and blood tests, which means I get ouchies. I can't tell you how many ouchies I've gotten. There have been too many to count. I also have to get blood transfusions every couple of months. My Mom and Dad take turns taking me to the hospital.

When I was little, I thought that my blood was dirty and that all kids had to get ouchies, but my Mom explained to me that my blood isn't dirty and not all kids have to get ouchies. The worst time I remember was when I had my first pain crisis. It felt like fire was burning inside of me. I was in the hospital for seven days. I cried a lot. All I wanted was for the pain to stop. When I finally went home from the hospital, I took about 12 medicines for a long time before I was better.

I don't want all the other kids in my class to know I have Sickle Cell Anemia. I've only told my best friend Amanda. Whenever I miss school and the kids ask my why I just tell them that I was sick. I never really explain why. It's not that I feel bad about having Sickle Cell, it's just that I don't want the other kids to treat me differently. That's why I love Camp Hole in the Wall—because when I go there people treat me like all the other kids. I don't have to talk about my disease and I can get it off my mind. I just have fun. What I like most about Camp Hole in the Wall is that the counselors are like parents, but they're also like kids—they take care of you but they also have lots of fun WITH YOU.

CHAPTER

We are in Paul's plane flying to an airfield near Lake Luzerne, New York. We have a rendezvous with Charles Wood, an eccentric, ebullient entrepreneur with businesses and holdings (the Great Escape amusement park among them) in the Lake George area. Charlie has visited the Hole in the Wall Gang Camp and he wants to start a similar camp in a location he has found that once housed a kind of dude-ranch facility.

Charlie meets us at the plane in a vintage white Rolls Royce, one of several highly valuable antique cars that are stored in his oversize garage. He tours us through the now defunct buildings and grounds that border the lake and include an indoor swimming pool. The buildings are nondescript, the rooms motel-style, but Charlie is bubbling with plans to enliven the place and make it more suitable for children. All the necessary camp elements are there, from kitchen and dining hall to auditorium and small lake, but it's a pretty far cry from the originality of our camp.

After that first year when we had only 288 children in attendance, not only were we operating at capacity, with over 1,000 campers each summer, but we had not been able to take all the qualified children who applied. Charlie's camp would be able to accommodate some of these kids, and in addition, since our age range is seven to fifteen, this Adirondack camp, which Charlie dubbed the Double H Hole in the Woods Ranch, would accept up to seventeen-year-olds. Also, as Charlie points out, the camp's nearby river could provide white-water rafting, and the topography permits skiing in the winter.

For us, it's part of our original dream plan, to build a camp in Connecticut that would encourage the formation of other camps around the country. Since cancer and related diseases are the most prevalent childhood afflictions, there is a great need to establish these facilities in as many areas as possible. Children were coming to our camp from all over the United States, Europe, and Asia, but they had to endure long journeys.

So we were happy to go along with Charlie and chipped in a couple of bucks for start-up costs. He assembled his own board of directors, but we helped him to train counselors and also provided some of our own staff to assist him in the early going. There then followed a concerted makeover effort, headed by camp director Max Yurenda. The ranch was made handicapped accessible. The old ski lodge was converted into an arts-and-crafts center. Tepees, campfire circles, a challenge course, a log chapel, and a petting zoo replete with goats, fawns, chickens, lambs, and other animals were all created on the 320-acre grounds, surrounded by the splendor of the Adirondack forests and lakes.

Once it got up to speed, the Hole in the Woods impacted the children much the same as the Hole in the Wall. "I've been to other camps," one youngster said, "where everybody was there for the same reason, but here it's different. At Double H, there are so many people with problems that are different than mine. Some people have physical problems, some are recovering from cancer, some have problems with their blood, but everyone learns from each other and we all get along together. Sometimes, when you see someone who looks different it's scary, but after a day or two you see that it's not that bad. You end up making friends with all kinds of people. The pool, the ropes, and everything are good, but not as much as the part of being together and growing stronger together."

Max Yurenda recalls one young girl, whom doctors had given only a short time to live, who was determined to attend the next camp session that was many months away. She astonished her doctors by willing herself to make it to that session. "We let her pick and choose her activities and she lit up every room with her smile. Sadly she passed away a short time after returning home, but to me that girl epitomizes what it means when we say that miracles happen here one child at a time."

A year later, we heard from a group in Florida that wanted to start a camp in central Florida. The impetus for that camp, destined to become the Boggy Creek Gang, originated with a remarkable fourteen-year-old girl named Jennifer Masi, who had attended the Hole in the Wall. When she was three years old, Jennifer had been diagnosed with neuroblastoma, a cancer of the adrenal glands and nervous system that causes multiple benign and malignant tumors. Surgery and therapy had brought some remission, but her first nine years had been plagued with sudden outbursts of tumors. She had endured seven operations.

Jennifer's parents were both practicing doctors of psychology, but eventually her father, Nick, abandoned his practice when he felt he was getting out of touch with the needs of his patients. "People would tell me their problems, and I would hear a voice in the back of my mind saying, 'That's not a problem . . . You want to hear a real problem?' In Jennifer's ninth year, she developed a ring of malignant tumors on her neck and from then on the fight really got hard—intensive chemotherapy, radiation, bone marrow transplant."

The Masis were able to help Jennifer in many ways, but not

with her deep feelings. "We tried counseling, but she was not able to talk to us about the cancer. Nothing worked until she spent two weeks at the Hole in the Wall Gang Camp with peers who shared her problems. The activity that benefited Jennifer the most wasn't any of the camp's programmed activities. It was the talks she had with her bunkmates, whispered confidences after lights-out. It was about their lives, their experiences, how they were coping. And I think what they were all really talking about was what would happen when they died. They can't talk about that at home. Your kids protect you as much as you protect them."

When Jennifer returned to her Florida home, she was bubbling over with enthusiasm and praise for her experience at the camp, and she immediately set about trying to convince anyone who would listen that a camp like Hole in the Wall should be built near her home in Fort Lauderdale. One of those who listened and was won over was her neighbor, David Horvitz, vice president of WLD Enterprises. "She would come by," Horvitz recalls, "and lobby me for it. 'You're rich, Mr. Horvitz, you could get us started.' I never met another kid like her, but then I never met another kid who was dying." Horvitz gave Jennifer $500,000 as seed money, and the project was on its way. But Jennifer was not destined to see it reach fruition.

She died shortly after her fourteenth birthday, but just before her death, she wrote this poem:

A dolphin swimming through an endless sea,
Struggling through each new obstacle . . .
Scared, worried, unsure of what's to come.
Tough, though,
Fighting, fighting,

Until one day she just couldn't anymore.
She wished to be in a place where she didn't have to fight
every inch.
And her wish was granted.

From the beginning there were problems that all our neo-phyte camps have faced—an inexperienced board, difficulties with land purchase, architecture, funding—but we never wa-vered in our cooperation and our conviction that the camp would be built. We made more than a dozen trips down to Florida, attending board meetings, trying to smooth over the rough patches, giving them the benefit of our experience, and providing operating funds. At one point, Paul was personally on the hook for a bundle.

On one occasion, we flew down to inspect a site that the board had chosen; in fact, they had already applied for a mort-gage. The land's most attractive feature was that it had several streams running through it, which fed a large, attractive lake. Upon inquiry, however, we discovered that the U.S. Army Corps of Engineers was planning to divert the streams, which meant, of course, that the property would eventually be without streams or lake.

Despite the fumbling and bumbling of those in charge, the Masis continued to press forward on Jennifer's behalf. They en-listed Dr. Arlan Rosenbloom, chief of pediatric endocrinology at Shands Hospital at the University of Florida in Gainesville, and Whitfield Palmer, president of MFM Industries in Ocala, who was just completing a term as chairman of a state business or-ganization, the Florida Council of 100. Palmer, in turn, brought several of those business leaders into the burgeoning organiza-tion, and this is the group that eventually came to us with the plan for the Boggy Creek Camp. We put up a million bucks and PL recruited his friend Ted Forstmann, a Wall Street investor who specializes in corporate takeovers. Forstmann matched our million and pledged to raise a million more.

In the meantime, Palmer had flown to Tampa to induce General Norman Schwarzkopf, who was himself a survivor of surgery for prostate cancer, to become a cofounder. David Horvitz flew the General and Palmer in his private plane to the Hole in the Wall, where they met with Newman and saw first-hand how the camp was interacting with its afflicted children. When, at the end of his visit, visibly moved by what he saw, the General signed on, PL and Hotch knew right then and there that Boggy Creek was destined to become a reality.

"The group of children I saw that day," Schwarzkopf says, "were mostly from the inner city. There they were—horseback riding, going up in hot air balloons, participating in a pandemo-nium of dancing and singing. It was absolute chaos—and that's what it should be. I thought, here's a sick child from the bleak inner city who is doing things he never would have had a chance to do. Some of them are going to die, yet, when I saw them, they were just being kids. That's what it's all about.

"It occurred to me that if a child undergoes chemotherapy and loses his hair, he'll be the odd man out in regular camp or school and will be known as 'the kid without hair.' At this camp, hair or no hair, no one cares.

"Once when I was traveling I stopped in Jacksonville to visit a pediatric hospital where I ran into one of the kids I had met at a cancer camp. Her name was Heather, and she was having a bone marrow transplant. When this happens, the immune sys-tem is reduced to nothing so it can accept the bone marrow. The kids who go through this ordeal stay in isolation for months, and only one person at a time is allowed in the room. So they wrapped me in a gown and surgical mask, and I walked in to visit her. Heather was curled up in the fetal position, just staring off in the middle of nowhere.

"But when she saw me, she sat up in bed and started talking to me—and what she wanted to talk about was CAMP. She told me about the friends she had made, what she had done, all the memories she held onto—we had a wonderful talk. Camp had been great for me, too. I had thought I would go there and be the big general and cheer these kids up, but I had walked away realizing they had cheered me up with their energy and zest for living.

"When I walked out of Heather's room about a half hour later, her mother threw her arms around me and started crying. She told me I was the only person Heather had talked to in six weeks. And that's when it dawned on me just how much camp had really meant to Heather. Camp had been her oasis of normalcy—her escape from the prison of her disease.

"In a world filled with hospital wards, sick rooms, nurses, and antiseptics, camp had been a place where she could run around and have fun like any other ordinary kid.

"We lost Heather, but at least she got the chance to be a kid in a summer camp, and it was something she looked forward to every year of her short life. That's why I wanted Boggy Creek to happen—for all the Heathers who otherwise would never have a chance to have any fun."

On returning to Tampa, the general solicited $500,000 each from General Mills and Outback Steakhouse, and Palmer took over as chairman of the board. A search for land led the group to Florida Hospital in Orlando, which owned a 230-acre forested area in Cassia, near Orlando, with two lakes, surrounded by undeveloped land. Palmer and his cohorts induced the hospital's officials to give them the land for Boggy Creek. Palmer assembled an influential board that included Publix Super Markets president Mark Hollis, Orlando hotelier Harris Rosen, Orlando Magic general manager Pat Williams, and New York Yankees' principal owner George Steinbrenner.

By January 1995, over $13 million had been raised, more than enough to get the buildings up and running. At the end of the first summer of operation, in 1996, at a dedication ceremony, Newman lauded Whit Palmer, "who at some considerable expense to other personal interests picked up this little ailing feller, dressed him in a snappy pair of shorts and shoes, pointed him in the right direction, and simply orbited him so that we could all applaud, pitch in, and keep him airborne."

Following the example set by the Hole in the Wall, some of the construction costs were defrayed by generous contributions. Pharmacia and Upjohn Pharmaceuticals donated the landscaping, planting new trees and shrubs and providing medical equipment; Darden Restaurants (owner of Red Lobster and The Olive Garden) designed the kitchen and covered the cost of its construction; the Orlando Magic Youth Foundation donated costly equipment for the recreation area; and Universal Studios funded the building of a theater. Other significant contributions came from the Outback Steakhouse Corporation, Sea World, and the General Mills Restaurants.

PL contacted Augustus Busch, who had given so generously to the Hole in the Wall, and again he came through. He met Paul at an airport lounge, arriving with his checkbook in his hand, prepared to fork over a check with enough digits to cover the considerable cost of the dining room.

The Boggy Creek Gang Camp is significantly larger than the

Hole in the Wall, and the mild weather enables it to be open all year long, with sessions for hemophilia, sickle cell, epilepsy, cystic fibrosis, diabetes, asthma, pulmonary diseases, arthritis, HIV/AIDS, cancer, heart and kidney diseases, as well as for children requiring ventilator assistance. The camp opened in 1996 and through 2002 has served 18,782 children.

In 1992, Paul visited a site in County Kildare, southern Ireland, twenty-five miles outside Dublin, which had once been the five-hundred-acre estate of Elizabeth Arden, who had ceded it to the Irish government. The centerpiece was a beautiful twelfth-century manor house; there were also two Gothic quadrangles that housed dozens of horse stalls. Paul fell in love with the place as a possible Hole in the Wall site, a captivating location with a medieval bent to it, knights and maypoles and jousting and all that.

As usual, PL was gung-ho to get under way and the board of the Hole in the Wall gave him its prompt approval. He met with the prime minister of Ireland, Paul Reynolds, who invested the embryonic camp with a ninety-nine-year lease for one annual Irish pound. PL then enlisted the cooperation of Anthony O'Reilly, chairman of the H.J. Heinz Company, and together they posted close to $3 million to get the project off the ground. A board was assembled and architectural changes planned, with much enthusiasm all around, but after that initial flurry, it became apparent that practically nothing was being accomplished on the Irish side of the Atlantic. It was at that point, with our ardor for this new camp beginning to flag, that Paul contacted Bob Forrester, who is a partner in a firm that works with non-profits.

"Paul asked me to go to Barretstown," Forrester says, "and assess the situation. It didn't take me long to get back to him. This is now 1994, cabins are being built, sick kids are going to show up in about eight weeks. Also, there are no employees, none.

"So I told Paul, it was either shift into emergency gear or fold, knowing in advance that Paul being Paul, he would rev up the engine. The most important thing was to staff the camp, and this was accomplished by sending an experienced team from Hole in the Wall. The highly qualified program director, Beverly Moore, became the camp director, accompanied by Charlotte Werner, who ran the Hole in the Wall kitchen and would now do the same for the Barretstown Gang. But that first summer there was no dining hall, so a tent was erected outside the kitchen window from which food was dispensed. Tony O'Reilly's wife, Chris, became the temporary chairman of the board, and Gavin, one of the O'Reillys' twin sons, together with a friend supervised all the building construction. From our office, we sent over a young associate, Amy Hines, who lived in the castle for a year and helped to organize the project and solicit desperately needed contributions. Substantial amounts came from Anheuser-Busch; a consortium of pharmaceuticals assembled by Senator Chris Dodd; the Guinness Company; a considerable amount from Michael Smurfit; the Ford Motor Company—as a matter of fact, the dining hall was named

Henry's Place when it was discovered that Henry Ford had been born in Ireland."

But as important as any of these was the team of Hole in the Wall counselors who arrived, like emergency marines, a week before that first session. Blake Maher, a three-year Hole in the Wall veteran, was in that contingent:

"I and five other veteran counselors ('caras' as counselors are called in Ireland, the Gaelic word for 'friend') from the Hole in the Wall Gang Camp had been commissioned to go to Ireland to assist in setting up the summer program, plan an orientation, train the staff, and, finally, to live in the cabins with the campers.

"There were the everyday activities: early morning soccer (if you were so inclined), arts and crafts, theater, sports and games, fishing, outdoor hikes, and woodworking. And then there were the not-so-usual events: a medieval Quest where characters from Irish lore materialized out of the woods, leading the campers through a day-long search for the Pooka, a prankish spirit who had robbed Barretstown of its music. There were treasure hunts and carnivals and campouts, cabarets at the theater where campers strutted their considerable talents; there was even a surprise afternoon visit from Mel Gibson and a cast of costumed warriors making a film in a nearby town.

"But best were the spontaneous moments: the night our cabin decided to make a movie and spent the next three hours writing a script, stealing costumes, and filming late into the evening. Or the night we decided to have a Ceili, a traditional festival highlighted by Irish dancing, the Irish campers and caras leading the rest of us as we stumbled over our feet.

"All summer we Americans had been hearing horror stories

about what to expect in the last session. Teenagers from Dublin would never sing camp songs, we were told. They would readily tell us where to go before they would dress up in costumes and ridiculous hats. I wondered how different these kids could be from other inner-city kids and teenagers I had worked with at Hole in the Wall.

"And at first it seemed the predictions had been right. One cabin of girls did not talk for the first two days. They did not smile. They did not laugh. They rolled their eyes at us when we sang. They remained aloof and watchful. One boy in our cabin told me in no uncertain terms where I could go and what I could do with the camp. I hoped this wasn't an omen of things to come. For the most part, though, the boys were excited, eager to have a go at the thirty-foot tree-climbing course that Eric had built, or take part in the day-long canoe trip down the Barrow, a system of lochs and small waterfalls that Brendan O'Connell, a canoeist for the Irish Olympic team, would lead us on later that week. But the girls remained silent. A tension was building.

"And then one day, like too much water behind a dam, the girls who had been so quiet for so long broke loose. It is hard to know exactly what caused it. Maybe it had been a particularly rambunctious morning in the theater. Whatever the reason, bust loose they did. They sang. They danced. They took over the dining hall, leading songs and announcements after every meal. They dressed in costumes and wore their hair in outrageous styles they would never have worn mere days before. And in true teenage fashion, the boys followed suit. Every day, they became more outgoing, more outrageous, the fear of appearance long gone. Like their counterparts at the Hole in the Wall Gang Camp, these campers, children who had experienced the isolation of illness—most of whom had been through chemotherapy or radiation or bone marrow transplants—unlocked the key to camp. They began to understand that it could be whatever they made it. It was magic, if they let it be. And, best of all, it was theirs. It was a time, a place, no one could ever take away.

"At the final banquet, campers and caras dressed in medieval garb—gowns, cloaks, and robes—while goblets and wooden plates adorned the tables. When you looked across the room, it seemed as if we were a court from another better age that had somehow outwitted time. That last night, after the awards had been presented and we were all in our cabins, there was a feeling of something unfinished in the air. Lights flashed on. Music began blasting. Campers began to pour out of every cabin. We spent the next hour signing autograph books, singing, dancing, not mourning what was soon going to end but rather celebrating what we had at that moment. A true Irish celebration.

"But the next morning, there was no denying the fact that they were heading home. There were tears, more than I had ever seen at Hole in the Wall, pledges of friendship and letters, and hugs for everyone. No one, including the caras, wanted the session to end.

"What I feel," Blake says, "is that in my heart and mind I have a second home now, even if I never return. More importantly, there are hundreds of children in Ireland who do, too."

"Today," Forrester says, "Barretstown is in relatively good shape. They are building a solid board, and international benefactors like AIG, GlaxoSmithKline, Intel, Janssen Pharmaceuticals, Johnson & Johnson, and Xerox have helped European recruitment. This summer the staff, volunteer interpreters, chaperones, and counselors came from twenty-seven countries. In 1994, the first year, the camp served one hundred and twenty-four children. This past summer, there were over fifteen hundred."

A volunteer doctor, Paul M. Zeltzer, a neurooncologist from the United States, says, "I have seen with my own eyes, repeatedly, that ten days at Barretstown helped bring back the child who was there prior to this disruption in their life. Before they leave, I see a sparkle in their eyes or a radiance in their voices that was barely present on day one. They can do this because of the community that is Barretstown."

PL and Hotch are in Paris having an epicurean lunch to which they have been invited by a group of Parisians who are intent on starting a Hole in the Wall–type camp in France. This is the second time we have lunched with this group in the past two years; there have been many luncheons and discussions about what they plan to do with the property they have acquired from the government, a property called L'Envol ("Takeoff"), on the edge of the Fontainebleau forest, just south of Paris, a property with a lake, a nineteenth-century château, and numerous quarters for living and classrooms. It was built in 1867 as a private residence for the president of the petroleum company that became Shell, had once been a college for "young English gentlemen," and in 1942 was converted into an orphanage for the children of aviators killed in World War II.

But that need has long passed, and the government has consented to give a long-term lease to our luncheon group for the purpose of installing a camp there for children with life-threatening illnesses. This luncheon assemblage consists of perfectly nice people who have no understanding of what has to be done, nor, even if they understood, the capacity to do it. They regard their participation as honorary, believing that the government will substantially contribute to the operation, and what is needed beyond that they will get from Paul Newman and his associates.

Actually, PL and Hotch did attend a fancy dress dinner at the Ritz that rasied funds for the camp, but essentially the only regular funds would come from the government, which would only cover two-thirds of the cost of each child's stay at the camp.

When L'Envol finally did get under way, the luncheon board elected a retired general as president and an admiral as camp director, but they couldn't overcome the fact that there is no tradition of camps in France, nor is there a tradition of philanthropy. The government provides funds—why should we?

Eventually, the military men were relieved of their command and replaced by a man who had been the head of the American Hospital in Paris, Patrice Trearuer, who had all the right stuff. Hole in the Wall sent some of their key personnel, even our resident clowns, Kim and Therese Winslow, to organize the L'Envol staff, and provide them with seed money to help in adapting the building and grounds to suit a population of sick children. In keeping with the camp's name, the highlight of each ten-day session is a ride in a guided plane or a hot-air balloon.

But just when the camp appeared to be finding its identity, the board dismissed Patrice, and another period of uncertainty followed, exacerbated by a shortage of operating funds. However, an event occurred on September 17, 2001, that may turn everything around. A dedication of a medical center at the camp occurred on that Monday, with PL and Jacques Chirac, the president of France, in attendance. Chirac, who had not previously known about the camp, was very moved by the children and what the camp was doing for them. He spent three hours among the children, participating with them in some of their activities.

At the dedication that afternoon, he said, "To these children, with all my heart, I wish them the best in their lives, the best which this center can help them find. When we are ill, when we have to face problems, it's good to have techniques, science, and medicine. We need competent people. But we also need other things. And children are no exception. We need love. We need hope. And the great merit of this center is that it gives this love, it gives this hope which is key to the morale of children. We need other camps like this in France."

As a result of Chirac's visit, there is now widespread interest in L'Envol and perhaps other camps like it. The Minister of Justice has now visited L'Envol and is publicly discussing the possibility of drafting laws that will permit American-style philanthropy. The wife of the prime minister is also campaigning for this change, and the Minister of Health has endorsed the camp as better medicine than being confined to a hospital room. He is presently working on plans for a sister camp, probably in the Marseilles area.

Even the staid, tradition-bound medical profession has unbuckled and said that "the camp is serious medicine, unlike the medicine we're used to—cutting kids and confining them to hospitals—this concept of palliative medicine, this whole area of respite helps a great deal."

L'Envol now has a new director and a reconstituted board that is bringing a fresh enlightenment to the camp's present and future needs. And one thing is for sure—true to Gallic tradition, L'Envol will continue to have the best cuisine of any of our camps.

There are new Hole in the Wall camps currently in various stages of development. The Painted Turtle Camp, located near Palmdale, California, is nearing completion and will receive its first children in 2004. It owes its existence to the devotion of Page Adler, who was a volunteer for two years at the Hole in the Wall in Connecticut.

"My interest in working with sick children," Page says, "goes back to the time I was living in New York and going to NYU. While at school I was volunteering at the Sloan-Kettering onco-logical section for children, primarily those receiving bone mar-row transplants. I heard about a camp that Paul and Hotch were opening in Connecticut for children with cancer. I had known Hotch for a long time—he was close friends with my stepfather, Jerry Wexler, and, in fact, had induced Jerry to donate funds to build the camp's tennis courts—and through Hotch I arranged to volunteer at the new camp. During my two years volunteering I formed a lasting friendship with Wendy Cook, the unit leader, who was attending medical school at Stanford University. Even while I pursued an acting career—I was in soaps and later had a continuing role in the television series *Fame*—I continued to volunteer at hospital units for afflicted children.

"I moved to Los Angeles, got married, had children, and on my way home from the hospital with my second child, I remember thinking that I really wanted to go back to working with sick children, and it occurred to me what a thrill it would be to build a camp like Hole in the Wall for afflicted children on the West Coast. That very night I phoned Wendy, who had just finished her internship, and even though she had been offered a very desirable fellowship and an opportunity to join a lucrative private practice, she turned down both opportunities and pledged herself to sharing my dream.

"The first thing out of the box, I naively began looking for a site for the camp. I found one in Santa Barbara, a tract of land with a lake that was owned by Jane Fonda, who had it up for sale for five million. It had once been a well-appointed camp for railroad executives. It so happened that Paul was about to start a movie in Hollywood and he had rented a house in Malibu that was adjacent to mine. Hotch was there to visit and they both went with me to inspect the Fonda property. We tried to negotiate the asking price with Jane, but she would not budge from her five million. At this point Hotch suggested that I might benefit from some professional guidance and put me in touch with Bob Forrester."

"I went out to the coast to meet with Page," Forrester says, "who was thinking of taking out a loan to buy the Fonda property. I said, here's my advice: Stop. You cannot acquire land or proceed in any other way until you have raised the capital to pay for it, otherwise you will become a hostage. If that property is right, it will still be there. What you have to do is make sure that you build something that works the moment it opens. That's what happened with the other camps. Children-wise they were doing beautifully, but they were financially wounded. If this is right to do, it'll get done. You have Newman and Hotchner behind you, you've got your own experience, and slowly you'll work everything out."

"It was wonderful advice," Page says. "Wendy came to join me—she had been volunteering her doctor services at the Hole in the Wall. We began assembling a board and soliciting donations, but it was tough sledding."

Forrester says, "I told Page to forget about big-name Hollywood people who lend their names but don't attend board meetings or help with fund-raising. I told her to seek out people who want to get involved and who have a conscience about giving money for a great cause like this."

Following his advice, Page began to accumulate sizeable donations, and she recruited a board of dedicated noncelebrity people. It was at this point that her husband, Lou, heard about a foreclosure on a mobile home park, a 173-acre site with its own 23-acre bass-filled lake, located sixty miles north of Los Angeles. Now Page and Wendy were in a position where they could acquire the land and build a state-of-the-art camp. In the spring of 2004, the Painted Turtle, with an organic gardening theme, will welcome its first group of children. The California Children's Hospital Association has identified 17,500 children in the state who have moderate to severe illnesses that preclude their attendance at regular camps. It is this group that the Painted Turtle will serve.

"As a volunteer at the Hole in the Wall Gang Camp," Page says, "I was initially overwhelmed by the magic that transformed the children. Only later did I realize that the real magic was in how much I came away with. What a gift. Now I hope this camp will be a meaningful gift to these children."

Also nearing completion and scheduled to open in June 2004 is the Victory Junction Gang Camp, founded by the race car driver Kyle Petty and his wife, Pattie, in honor of their son, Adam, who was killed in an accident on the racetrack. Victory Junction is located in the town of Randleman, in the Piedmont Triad of North Carolina, on seventy-five acres surrounded by hardwood forests. There are thirty-six buildings already constructed in a setting that will embody a racing theme, with the sights, sounds, look, and feel of a racetrack. The campers will enter the camp through a tunnel that will lead them over a starting line into the world of racing, which is epitomized by the racetrack-shaped core campus. The majority of children will come from Virginia, North Carolina, and South Carolina.

NASCAR has designated the camp as one of its sponsored charities, which has been a boon to fund-raising and to building public awareness of the camp's mission through a media campaign that reaches across all of NASCAR's licensed media.

The Pettys first became interested in starting a camp in North Carolina after Pattie visited the Boggy Creek Gang Camp in Florida. They approached Paul about cofounding the camp with them because, Kyle says, "We didn't want to reinvent the wheel. We spent three years with people from his camps, learning what mistakes had been made, and what we could do better. We named it Victory Junction after the winning circle at a racetrack, and we made that the overall theme of the camp. Adam became very interested in the project, and the week before he died he had made arrangements to buy the property that would be the campsite.

"After Adam died, as we struggled with our terrible loss, we cancelled the loan he had taken out on the property. But searching for a way to make sense of the tragedy, we eventually decided to channel our grief into reviving his dream of building an extraordinary camp. We needed something to help us through the healing process and the camp became a labor of love for Pattie and me. We thought this camp could be a testament to how Adam lived his life. He touched more people than we could have imagined. Adam lived his life how the Bible says—it is not what you say but how you live. He walked the talk.

"Unfortunately, when we decided to go forward with Victory Junction, we found that the property Adam had chosen had been sold. Instead, Adam's grandparents, Richard and Lynda, donated seventy-five acres of land from the family property in his memory. The cost of building the camp, with its thirty-six buildings, would be $24 million, but from the beginning my conviction was—and I don't say this with any arrogance or conceit—if I said we're going to make it happen, then it will happen. Maybe that's why we're hardheaded and race cars. I don't think failure is an option for us in anything we do, but especially not for this camp.

"There are certain people now involved with Victory Junction who, when I'm around them, make me feel like Adam's also here. I feel his closeness because of the relationships he had with them, and that we had together. When I walk on this piece of property that's growing with buildings, that's how I feel. And I pray that never goes away. When I walk around these grounds, I feel Adam is with us."

כפר נהר הירדן
Jordan River Village
قرية نهر الأردن

The Jordan River Village camp has the distinction of having been accepted as a member of the Hole in the Wall Gang Association even though no buildings or facilities have yet been constructed. This sixty-one-acre site beside the Jordan River is in a secluded, safe area in the Lower Galilee, high above the Sea of Galilee, on the Israeli side of the river, directly across from Jordan. The guiding lights of this camp are Marilyn and Murray Grant, who live in Tampa but for many years have frequently been in Israel. It was Marilyn who, in 1999, read a Hole in the Wall brochure and immediately knew that such a camp serving critically ill children from Israel, Jordan, Lebanon, and Palestine would be wonderful for afflicted children in this troubled area.

The Grants came to us with a vision and an enthusiasm that couldn't be denied, and even though millions had to be raised and medical and ethnic cooperation obtained, we submitted their request to the board, which was so moved by the objectives of the proposed camp that it granted membership on the basis of promises and dreams rather than reality.

"We had a great ally in Simon Peres," Murray Grant says, "and we also got a ringing endorsement from Prince Mired Raad Zeid Al-Hussein when we visited him in the Royal Palace in Jordan. "This camp," the Prince said, "I believe will not only bring tremendous joy and happiness to children faced with severe hardship, but will also serve to cement the bonds of friendship and trust between our people on both sides of the river Jordan."

Paul expressed a similar expectation when he wrote to the Grants in May 2000, "I share your hope that, in the future, this camp can reach out to children from throughout the eastern Mediterranean area and serve to enhance the efforts toward peace in your region."

The Grants have assembled a prestigious multinational board, chaired by the acclaimed actor Chaim Topol. Fifteen leading hospitals, including Schneider Children's Medical Center, Sheba Medical Center, Dana-Ichilov Children's Hospital, the Soroka University Medical Center, and Hadassah Medical Organization, have pledged their support, along with other medical and professional organizations and the Israeli Minister of Health. Forty-three prominent Israeli and Arab physicians have formed a medical committee.

It has taken two years to obtain all the permits needed to operate, permissions from religious, environmental, archeological, and government groups, but the Grants say the time has come to put shovels in the ground and erect on the shore of the River Jordan a place where suffering children can find an interlude of respite.

Waiting in the wings, having applied for admission to the Association, is the Over the Wall Gang camp in the U.K. Unlike the other camps, it does not have a campus of its own but leases private school facilities during the summer months when the schools are out of session. Started in August 1999, it has served children with cancer and other life-threatening diseases from England, Scotland, and Wales. Its admission to the Association is contingent on a collaboration agreement with Barretstown on recruitment and fund-raising.

In the meantime, Over the Wall prospers, significantly increasing its enrollment, year by year. It has a first-rate chief executive in Jan Nicholas, and a varied and energetic board. It has also achieved strong rapport with its children and their parents.

A London parent of one of the campers writes, "One night when Zoë and the other girls in her room couldn't get to sleep they decided to all sit on the floor in a circle and tell each other their problems. Zoë told them that she had spina bifida and that some things inside her body didn't work. Another little girl had diabetes and three of Zoë's friends had a brain tumor. They discussed how many operations they had had and then they went on to talk about secrets. Zoë didn't say any more and I didn't ask what those secrets were. It made me feel upset thinking about these little nine-year-olds having this conversation and yet at the same time it must have been very special for them all to be able to do this. Thank you for inviting Zoë to camp. She has benefited from going in so many ways."

For children with serious illnesses
Association of Hole in the Wall Camps
laughter is the best medicine.

The most ambitious of all our camp endeavors is the new initiative in Africa. As to be expected when PL is involved, the program had an accidental beginning. Paul had gone on safari with Ray LaMontagne and members of their families. On their return, during an eight-hour layover in Johannesburg, they had made an appointment to visit Nelson Mandela. But Mandela could not receive them because he was too ill from the cancer treatment he was receiving. As an alternative, in order to pass the time, the guide suggested that Paul and Ray meet with Colin Bell, the CEO and owner of Wilderness Safaris.

Out of that casual meeting came the plan to use Bell's safari facilities for children's camps during the safari off-season of December and January, very hot months when the children are out of school. In view of the fact that Colin Bell had to keep staff on during those months even though there were no safaris, the facilities would be able to take care of a limited number of children.

But a structure had to be assembled for selecting the children and transporting them, and training staff and doctors to take care of them. UNICEF estimates that there are more than 100,000 orphans (as a result of their parents dying from AIDS) in Botswana and Namibia, which is where the first Hole in the Wall camps operated last year. A major problem was having to establish the program in at least three languages, Setswana, English, and a mix of Bantu languages. Another complication was the fact that most children do not have medical records. Also, in many places, such as the Okavango Delta, the only way to get the children to camp is by airplane, and the counselors have had to merge different social and cultural approaches to child development to make the camps appealing to the youngsters.

Mwenya Kabwe, a native of Zambia, assistant program director at the Hole in the Wall, has also been an associate for the Africa Program from the beginning. This is from a report she sent to the board of directors:

Among the less typical hurdles of creating a camp program in Southern Africa is working with the fact that the idea of sending kids away to the middle of nowhere to hang out with a group of strangers is hardly a cultural phenomenon. Not to mention the necessity of carrying a shovel to the football field every day to shovel the buffalo dung before we could play. On another hand it can also be described as the ultimate test in patience and creativity as we put our energies toward some of the most inspiring work in one of the most breathtakingly beautiful parts of the world.

Kids are kids everywhere you go, they have food allergies, love playing with water, enjoy being entertained by goofy adults, can tell when adults are insincere and have an aversion to going to bed on time. A little less typical was the 18-year-old camper who arrived at Camp Vumbura with her 10-year-old nephew, 8-year-old niece, and 10-month-old baby. This strikingly beautiful Bushman family arrived with the clothes on their backs and no command of either of the languages we had been using (English or Setswana). We track down a local guide who speaks a similar dialect to theirs and convince the mother to give the baby a bath. Water in their village, we find out, is a precious commodity, arriving in drums to a central point every couple of weeks if they are lucky. Travel in and out of Camp Vumbura is expensive and by plane. We arrange for the next flight to arrive that evening to bring beads, dry food, fruit, diapers and baby clothes. The baby was cared for in shifts by all of us between game drives, soccer, cooking, talent shows, wildlife videos and jenga competitions.

It was the last day of the last session at Mokolodi and we had spent the morning bidding tearful goodbyes to our last group of kids. We had packed up our remaining supplies and were reminiscing about our two favorite kids from the session, Bradly and Khumo, the closest we had come all summer to any real behavioral issues. These were a pair of ten-year-old kids who lived on the street most of the time because their family homes were overflowing with other relatives. They came to the last session of camp and spent the week testing the patience of every staff member. To celebrate the end of the project and congratulate ourselves on a hard job very well done, we threw ourselves a barbeque that evening. At about 7pm the cell phone of the Director of the Education Centre rings, and it's the front gate of Mokolodi. They are calling to inform us that there is a child at the gate wanting to come in. Three of us drive to the gate and there is Khumo, standing there, barefoot, in a T-shirt with his yellow bandana crooked on his head the way he had worn it all session long. His story is that his van left him behind in the morning. He says that he got out, just as they were leaving, to go to the bathroom and when he came back, everyone had left and he has been wandering around the nature reserve all day looking for someone he knows. Of course we are horrified at the news that we "lost" a child and didn't even know he has been wandering around 10,000 acres inhabited by African wildlife. Two counselors make Khumo a big plate of food as I get on the phone to the director of the organization that picked him up. It turns out that Khumo was in fact dropped at his house, a two-hour drive from Mokolodi, at 10:30am that morning. What had in fact happened was that he had changed his shirt, taken his shoes off for some reason, and made his way back to Mokolodi to come back to camp.

Despite the obstacles, in December 2002, our first year in Africa, six hundred children attended the Hole in the Wall camps in Botswana and Namibia. That number will be doubled this coming year, and additional camps will open in Rwanda, Sierra Leone, and Kenya. "The number of children served from over 100,000 orphans and street children may seem insignificant but actually it's a step forward," says Steve Nagler, director of New Program Development for the Association of Hole in the Wall Camps. "I like to tell the story that I read in a book, *The Star Thrower* by Loren Eisley. It's about a man who sees a person on the beach throwing starfish back into the sea that have washed up on the shore, and are dying. The observer says, 'There are millions of starfish washed up on the beach. What you are doing can't possibly make a difference.' The starfish thrower bends down, throws another one back and says, 'It made a difference to that one.'

"To give you one example: in the town of Maun, Botswana,

the dusty last stop on the way to the Okavango Delta, ten young adolescent boys came to our first camp from a program for street kids. None of them were attending school. After completing our program, eight out of the ten went back to school full time. At another camp, twelve out of fifteen did the same thing. What is fascinating is that the kids in Africa react just the same way as the kids in Connecticut. They start off the week quiet, shy, even skeptical. By the end of the week they have opened up like the flowers you see in stop-action nature films. They're loud and raucous and full of life, ready to face the challenges of their situation with renewed spirit and hope."

Plans are under way to enlarge the operation in Africa. Working with Wilderness Safaris, Hole in the Wall is creating a camp at Mkambati, Eastern Cape Province, on a 45,000-acre game and nature preserve along the Wild Coast of the Indian Ocean. The camp will be on the site of a former leprosarium.

CHAPTER 22

Not all of our camp activity has occurred without certain reverses. Despite a careful search for our first camp director, the man we eventually chose had serious shortcomings, so serious he had to be dismissed midway during the summer (Doc Pearson replaced him temporarily). We did what we thought was thorough research, but certainly it was not. The man turned out to be psychotic. That nobody got seriously hurt or worse during that period is just another manifestation of extraordinary luck. We must have had our hearts in the right place.

Another reversal was a new camp, the Buffalo Prairie Gang Camp in Peoria, Illinois, which ran into such problems that, although only partially built, it had to be shut down before it was completed.

And then there was what happened in London in 1989. Hotch had been interviewed on the BBC about Newman's Own (we were in U.K. grocery stores) and the Hole in the Wall Gang Camp, as a result of which Hotch received a communication from the Trustee of an organization called The Duke's Trust, the Trustee writing on behalf of the Duke of Manchester, who was one of the dukes who belonged to the Trust. In his letter, the

Trustee, Paul Vaughn SP, explained that the Duke desired to meet and discuss the possibility of sponsoring, on behalf of the Trust, a camp like ours in the U.K.

Vaughn identified the Dukes of the Trust as:

The Duke of Norfolk, KG, CB, CBE, MC.
Earl Marshall and Hereditary Marshall and
Chief Butler of England; Premier Duke and Earl.

The Duke of St. Albans
Hereditary Grand Falconer of England;
Hereditary Registrar, Court of Chancery.

The Duke of Argyll,
Chief of Clan Campbell;
Hereditary Master of the Royal Household, Scotland.
Admiral of the Western Coast and Isles.
Keeper of the Great Seal of Scotland.

The Duke of Manchester,
Viscount Mandeville,
Baron Mantagu of Kimbolton.

The Duke of Wellington, MVO, OBE, MC.
Prince of Waterloo (Netherlands).
Marquess of Torres Vedras and
Duke of Vitoria (Portugal).
Duke of Ciudad Rodrigo.

We had lunch with the Duke and Duchess in London that summer to explore the possibility of a camp outside London.

The Duke, an affable, natty, loquacious gentleman, explained that such a camp would be in the purview of the Trust, and he proposed that we advance to him, on behalf of the Trust, the sum of $200,000 as seed money to get the camp started. With that many Dukes behind it, we felt it had a very good chance of fruition and since it was the policy of Newman's Own to provide our foreign markets with that country's profits for their charities, we decided to use the U.K. profits for the payment to the Duke's Trust.

It may well be that when we got into this with the Duke, we had sniggely thoughts about the possibility of getting our own Dukedom—Newman's Own Duchy-on-the-Thames, or at least getting rapped on the shoulder blade by the Queen and made a couple of honorary knights. Sir PL, Sir Hotch—not a bad ring to it. Rubbing elbows with Duchesses and Earls. Royal Olive Oil and Vinegar Purveyors to the Queen.

We signed relevant documents and went to London for the express purpose of meeting with the Duke of Manchester and giving him the proposed $200,000. But that's when Lady Luck, that good old sidekick of ours, once again kicked us in the butt. When PL reached in his pocket for the check, it wasn't there. Ol' PL is noted for lapses like that because in his very busy life he often overruns things and vice versa.

So the following afternoon, after his lunch with a London friend, Hotch planned to deliver the $200,000 check to the Duke at his hotel. In the course of that lunch, Hotch mentioned to his friend John that we were funding the Duke of Manchester for the purpose of starting a camp in England.

A look of immense incredulity suffused John's face. "The Duke . . . of *Manchester*!"

"Yes."

"Two . . . hundred . . . thousand . . . dollars?"

"That's right."

A wave of laughter rose up from John's belly, an unrestrained full-throttled guffaw, his face reddening as he choked over his laughter, tears coursing down his cheeks. "Two . . . thou . . . the duke . . ." He coughed laughter into his handkerchief.

"No, you're not," he finally managed to say, as he dried his cheeks and blew his nose.

"Not what?"

"Forking over two hundred thou U.S. to the Dupe of Manchester."

"You say 'Dupe'?"

"My dear fellow, you may be awed by this Duke business, but get this picture—bloke on the docket at the Old Bailey on criminal charges that he and some confederates tried to obtain thirty-eight thousand pounds from the National Westminister Bank in Streatham, down south from here, and what do they post as security for the cash? American bonds that are counterfeit. So while this bloke is in criminal court, he gets word that his brother or uncle or some such has kicked off and this indicted criminal, this black sheep of the family, is now the Duke of Manchester. All over the papers."

"This is my Duke?"

"Your very Duke. His barristers somehow maneuver to get him acquitted, but I had a helluva laugh over what the judge said at the end of the trial: 'On a business scale of one to ten, the Duke is one or less—and even that flatters him.'"

PL had located the missing check that had mysteriously appeared at the bottom of his shaving kit, but we were not about to hand over $200,000 to a Duke who was rated one or less. Instead we hired a snoop, one of those Fleet Street ferrets who snout out the dark and scurrilous items that they feed to London's hungry tabloids. Our snoop discovered that the Duke's Trust existed in name only, and that the Duke's ancestral seat at Kimbolton had been sold, which meant that the Duke of Manchester had no property, in fact was the only Duke listed who had no territory. Needless to say, the $200,000 transfer did not take place, and although constantly pursued by the Duke and his cohorts, who exuded an overwhelming passion for helping sick children, we avoided any further contact.

But our snoop, true to his calling, continued to send us bulletins about the Duke. In 1996 came snoop word that the Duke had once again been hauled into court, this time in Florida, where he was accused, along with four others, of defrauding the Tampa Bay Lightning ice hockey team. The Duke had been made honorary chairman of the team in 1991, on the basis of promising to raise $25 million for them in bank loans. The money was supposed to come from a Dublin company, Link International, whose chairman was the Duke, with a fee of $2.5 million being paid to the Duke and Link. But shortly after the Tampa Bay Lightning had advanced $50,000 in fees, Link went out of business. At the trial, the Duke's lawyer said his client was "more of a dupe than a duke," that the Duke was the perfect fall guy, and that every time he was involved in the transactions someone was handing him a drink. "He was used," his lawyer pleaded, "because he's gullible, he's vain, he's foolish, but none of that is a crime." The Duke did not take the witness stand and was straight-out convicted on four counts of fraud. He served twenty-eight months in the state penitentiary, where he ran the laundry. He died in August 2002, under mysterious circumstances. And with that bulletin, our snoop signed off.

☞ These few instances of bad luck were more than allayed by high-risk projects that, thanks to good luck and a wellspring of generosity, paid off handsomely. Two years after the Hole in the Wall Gang Camp opened, we built a remarkable theater, and it occurred to us that we could stage a fund-raiser for the camp if we put on a show in September after the camp closed. What we had in mind was a kind of revue entertainment, using a few of the children along with Hollywood and Broadway stars, but, it was pointed out, the camp is three hours from New York, and the theater, at capacity, only seats 280, there would be no TV or press, so how would we induce any performers to participate? As a matter of fact, how would we persuade people to spend $1,000 a ticket and drive all the way to the remote reaches of Connecticut? Our plan was to serve a hearty lunch under a big tent, and stage an auction followed by an hour show that Hotch would write and produce.

We decided to invite a dozen stars in the hopes that two or three might say yes. Besides Joanne and Paul, the list included Judy Collins, Phylicia Rashad, Kathie Lee Gifford, James Naughton, Barbara Rush, B. D. Wong, Savion Glover, Jason Robards, Cy Coleman, dancers from *Cats*, and that incomparable New York balladeer, Bobby Short. To our amazement and consternation, they all accepted. What's more, we sold every seat in the house. The show ran over two hours and the auction was a big success—Kathie Lee Gifford even auctioned off the necklace she was wearing.

In the fourteen years of these September galas, we have had remarkable performances from: Danny Aiello (twice), *Sesame Street*'s Big Bird, Kevin Kline (twice), Gene Shalit (three times), George Shearing, Alec Baldwin (four times), Rosemary Clooney, Tony Randall (eleven times), Amy Grant (three times),

Kim Basinger, Michael Bolton, Ann Reinking (four times), Melanie Griffith (twice), Joan Rivers (twice), Glenn Close, Marisa Tomei, Bill Irwin, Whoopi Goldberg (twice), Harry Belafonte (twice), Nathan Lane, Julia Roberts, Carole King (six times), *Stomp*, Christopher Reeve, Chita Rivera, Isaac Stern, Phoebe Snow (twice), Jack Klugman, Lillias White, Willie Nelson, Rosie O'Donnell, Robin Williams, Eartha Kitt, Jerry Seinfeld, Joshua Bell, Cy Coleman (eleven times), Kristen Chenoweth, Michael J. Fox, Gregory Hines, Jerry Stiller, Ben Vereen, Mikhail Baryshnikov, plus jazz bands, dance groups, gospel singers, acrobats (Anti-Gravity), and magicians—a galaxy of stars.

The children have performed in sketches and musical numbers with these stars, moments they cherish forever. And the performers say that the children have given them moments that they too will never forget.

For all these galas Hotch has cast Paul in a wild variety of roles, mostly in drag (he has been Tinkerbell, the Good Fairy, and a Miss America contestant), but he has actually enjoyed these embarrassments. All together, the fourteen galas have raised $11,187,490 for the camp and played to 4,300 people.

In November 2001 at Avery Fisher Hall in Lincoln Center, and a year later at the Kodak Theater in Hollywood, we staged two large-scale benefits for the camp, a concert dramatization Hotch wrote involving Hemingway's Nick Adams stories, Aaron Copland's original musical score, and chamber orchestras, the St. Luke's in New York and the Los Angeles Philharmonic in Hollywood. Once again, remarkable actors devoted themselves to the cause: in New York, the cast consisted of Danny Aiello, Alec Baldwin, Matt Damon, Brian Dennehy, Morgan Freeman, Philip Seymour Hoffman, Kevin Kline, James

Naughton, Paul Newman, Gwyneth Paltrow, Julia Roberts, Meryl Streep, and Joanne Woodward; in Hollywood, Paul, Joanne, Matt Damon, Brian Dennehy, Kevin Kline, and Julia Roberts repeated their roles, joined this time by Warren Beatty, Annette Bening, Danny DeVito, Danny Glover, Tom Hanks, Goldie Hawn, Jack Nicholson, Chris O'Donnell, Edward James Olmos, Gary Sinise, Mena Suvari, and Bruce Willis. In both performances, groups of campers participated. The result was that 6,400 people attended and $3,300,000 was raised for the camps.

To undertake events of this magnitude—the high-stakes gamble of filling 2,900 seats at Avery Fisher and 3,500 at the Kodak, with orchestra tickets going at $2,500 a pop—was but another instance of how Lady Luck has kept us in her sights.

CHAPTER

23

In 2002, our gross sales were $110 million, with an after-tax profit of $12 million, which we distributed to over two hundred charities. For 2003, profits for charity are projected to increase over 32 percent. Newman's Own now has seventy-seven different products produced by fifteen factories, thirteen in the United States, the other two in Australia and Scotland. A few years ago, although Advantage Foods was still functioning very well as our broker, we decided that the business had outgrown our ability to manage it, that we had reached a point where we no longer had the time or expertise to run it properly, so we replaced ourselves. We were looking for someone with good marketing skills, who could run a business, was intimately connected with the grocery business and really good with people; someone who could relate to the mercurial ways of Newman's Own.

We proceeded to interview a wide assortment of refugees from the food jungle—doughnut dominators, no-calories no-fat no-taste dairy executives, cereal big shots, marketing mavens, canned-good gurus; we even hired and quickly fired a business consultant who, as it turned out, needed a business consultant.

Eventually, through perseverance and tarot cards, in September 1997, we installed a good guy as COO, Tom Indoe, who had been an executive in sales and marketing for major food companies. He brought in Mike Havard as vice president for marketing, and Mark Tilly as director of special sales. Newman's Own stabilized and now we seem to be back on track. Through our Goodwill Alliance program, we have contributed to local charities via a network of brokers and retailers. We have also forged a "Partnership for Hunger Relief" with America's Second Harvest and the Ford Motor Company to provide food and trucks to distribute the food to twelve food banks around the country. In addition, we have set up a program to cooperate with Citymeals-on-Wheels.

As for our products, they multiply and prosper—in fact, there has been only one casualty, ice cream, which, ironically, was one of our best products. From the colorful graphics on the cartons to the racy names and legend, it had high promise, but we made the mistake of letting an outside company (the first and only time), Ben & Jerry's, produce and distribute it. They, in turn, turned over our distribution to Dreyer's, which also distributed their own ice cream, plus Ben & Jerry's and Starbuck's. We should have known that Dreyer's would quite understandably favor the promotion and sale of these established competitive products over ours, but by the time we came to realize that our ice cream was not getting into the markets, it was too late to do anything about it. Even though it is currently in limbo, we fully expect to reconfigure its manufacture and distribution and restore Obscene Vanilla Bean, Pistol Packin' Praline, and Giddy-Up Coffee, all bearing our ice cream legend:

In 1777, in the Alpine village of Uberotten, Baron "Buzz" Newman (The Original Newman from whence all subsequent Newmans sprung) was tending his herd of cows when a fierce, unforgiving ice storm flash-froze the entire herd and left them stark-stiff in their tracks. In the spring when the cows thawed, Buzz milked them like always. What came out Buzz sold as Iced Cream.

Every winter after that, Buzz froze all his cows stark-stiff in order to satisfy the growing demand for his Iced Cream. It was not until 1883 that Buzz's grandson, "Bubbles" Newman, the Rotter of Uberotten, invented the cuckoo clock and also hit upon the revolutionary idea of freezing the milk instead of the cows. He also created flavors by tossing in Alpine fruits like Elderberry, Youngerberry, and Berri-Berri. The current Newman is not only proud to carry on the family tradition but also honored to fulfill the exalted pledge of his ancestors: "100% COW! NO BULL!"

CHAPTER 24

"I really cannot lay claim to some terribly philanthropic instinct in my base nature," PL says. "It was just a combination of circumstances. If the business had stayed small and had just been in three local stores, it would never have gone charitable. It was just an abhorrence of combining tackiness, exploitation, and putting money in my pocket, which was excessive in every direction.

"Now that I'm heavily into peddling food, I begin to understand the romance of business—the allure of being the biggest fish in the pond and the juice you get from beating out your competitors. I would like to see the company reach $250 million in sales, and be able to support new philanthropic initiatives. We were a joke in 1982, but the joke has given away over $150 million so far—so we are a very practical joke. And the best part: we always thought the people on the other end of the checks would be the beneficiaries. But as with the exploitation—there's a kind of circularity here as well. A reciprocal trade agreement, so to speak.

"One thing that really bothers me is what I call 'noisy philanthropy.' Philanthropy ought to be anonymous, but in order for this to be successful you have to be noisy. Because when a shopper walks up to the shelf and says, 'Should I take this one or that one?' you've got to let her know that the money goes to a good purpose. So there goes all your anonymity and the whole thing that you really cherish. Publicize the generosity in order to become more generous. That's been the most difficult part of it. But overcoming that dichotomy has provided us with the means of bringing thousands of unlucky children to the Hole in the Wall Gang Camps.

"Since the Connecticut camp opened in 1988, a time when only 30 percent of the children who attended survived, medical progress has been phenomenal, especially in the field of bone marrow transplants; the result is that the percentages have been completely reversed—70 percent of those children who come to camp will now survive; but during the critical time of treatment and recovery we furnish them with much needed respite.

"Also, the number of children with HIV is decreasing precipitously in Connecticut. There have only been two or three children born in Connecticut with HIV in the last ten years. It is also thrilling to note that thirty-five of last summer's counselors were former campers who had overcome cancer and were now taking care of kids afflicted as they were. At the end of last summer's session, a counselor who had been a media major in college, on the basis of her experience at the camp changed her course of studies to pursue a medical career in pediatric oncology. And there was the doctor who had come to camp as a volunteer for a couple of weeks who said, 'I will never be able to practice medicine the way I used to. I will see a child as a child—I will never again think of him as a patient.'

"Last summer I was sitting next to a youngster at lunch, must have been fourteen or fifteen, who said it was his third summer at camp. He said he had been born with a brain tumor and had two or three serious operations that had so far saved his life. He had a history of fits and strokes, of spasms and headaches. He said his life was nothing but one headache after another—'until I come up here. I come up here, my headaches go away.'

"Another experience last summer—a marvelous African American girl who told me, 'Coming up here is what I live for, what I stay alive for during those miserable eleven months and two weeks is to come up here for the summer.'"

☛ That bottle of salad dressing that we concocted as a prank in Newman's old stable twenty-odd years ago has had a hell of a ride. Without realizing it, by being both stupid and stubborn we stuck to our guns, insisted on all-natural, no preservatives products, and in some small way caused an industry to change its ways. A business we ran by the seat of our pants, without plans or budgets, is now a significant player in the world's markets. A camp we built in Connecticut for sick children has now been duplicated for afflicted kids all over the world. A vision realized. Like the grain of sand in the oyster, it just grew, and for us, these camps are indeed the pearls.

So whatever it is, whatever it amounts to, whatever it does or doesn't do, we grabbed it by the shirttail and hung on. Sure makes a believer out of you.

APPENDIX

NEWMAN'S OWN CHRONOLOGY

- **Christmas 1980:** Paul Newman entices his longtime buddy A. E. Hotchner to accompany him in his basement, where they fill an endless collection of empty wine bottles with Newman's home-made salad dressing to be given as presents to Newman's friends and neighbors.
- **Spring 1981:** Newman gets the brilliant idea to bottle and sell his salad dressing in local gourmet shops. Hotch is sent out to hustle a manufacturer to produce Newman's recipe.
- **September 1982:** Newman's Own Salad Dressing is officially launched before a captive press group.
- Astounding first-year profits of $920,000. Paul immediately declares: "Let's give it all away to them what needs it."
- **February 1983:** Newman's Own Industrial Strength All-natural Venetian-style Spaghetti Sauce is introduced with grand fanfare, and Paul sings spaghetti song duet with Joanne Woodward.
- A total of $1 million in profits is generated from Newman's Own Salad Dressing, all of which is donated to charity.
- **July 1984:** Newman's Own Old Style Picture Show Popcorn is introduced with a media event at the Westport Historical Society. Newman, along with Molly and the Popcornettes, sing the praises of the popcorn.
- **1984 profits:** Over $2 million donated to charity. Newman's Own has sold 18,705,555 bottles of salad dressing and 8,371,726 jars of

spaghetti sauce. The profits to date total approximately $4 million, every penny of which has been given to deserving charities.

- **February 1985:** Another Newman's Own product pops up—Newman's Own Microwave Popcorn.
- **September 1986:** Paul Newman envisions his own charity—a camp for children with cancer. December 20, 1986, ground is broken for the Hole in the Wall Gang Camp.
- **August 1987:** Joanne Woodward divulges a secret recipe zealously guarded by seven generations of her Georgia family, and Newman's Own Old Fashioned Roadside Virgin Lemonade is born. Newman's startling disclosure is that the lemonade restores virginity! Scientists are amazed.
- **1987:** $5 million given to charity, $15 million to date.
- **June 29, 1988:** The Hole in the Wall Gang Camp opens in Ashford, Connecticut.
- **1989:** Newman's Own receives the Connecticut Governor's Laurel Award for responsible social involvement.
- **1989:** $7 million donated to charity, $28 million to date ($9.5 million to the Hole in the Wall Gang Camp).
- **1989:** Newman's Own receives the Council on Economic Priorities Award for Charitable Giving.
- **1990:** Two new products debut: Newman's Own Light Italian Dressing and a spicy pasta sauce, Bandito Diavolo.
- **1991:** A bevy of new products are introduced: Newman's Own Salsa, Light Microwave Popcorn, and Ranch Dressing.
- **June 1991:** Newman's Own and *Good Housekeeping* sponsor the first annual recipe contest, which awards over $100,000 to the winners' favorite charities.
- **1993:** In conjunction with Charles Wood, Newman helps start a sister camp, the Double H Hole in the Woods Ranch, in Lake Luzerne, New York.

- **April 1993:** Newman and Hotch are presented with Columbia University's Lawrence A. Wien Special Recognition Award for Outstanding Philanthropic Commitments.
- **June 1993:** Newman is named the 1993 Southern New England Entrepreneur of the Year for Social Responsibility.
- **October 1993:** The Culinary Oscars—Newman awards over $175,000 to the winners in the Third Annual Newman's Own and *Good Housekeeping* Recipe Contest.
- **March 1994:** Newman wins his third Oscar, the Jean Hersholt Humanitarian Award, for donating more than $56 million to charity through his Newman's Own food business and for his commitment to philanthropy.
- **February 1994:** Newman joins General Norman Schwarzkopf in breaking ground for the third Gang Camp, the Boggy Creek Gang Camp, in Lake County, Florida.
- **April 1994:** Bombolina (aka "The Intimate Companion Your Pasta Will Never Forget"), the fifth in the Newman's Own line of pasta sauces, is introduced. Three months later, Newman dons a toga and brews the latest in his line of all-natural dressings—Caesar. The label features Newman as Julius Caesar, replicated in a marble bust.
- **September 1994:** $200,000 is donated to the American Red Cross Rwandan Relief Fund to provide supplies and other vital assistance to the thousands of victims.
- **January 1995:** Newman announces 1994 charity donations of nearly $6 million—100 percent of his after-tax profits from Newman's Own. This brings the total donated since the company's inception to almost $62 million.
- **April 1995:** Supporting *USA Weekend*'s "Make a Difference Day," the annual community service event participated in by over one million people, Newman pledges $100,000 to the top fifty honorable mention winners on behalf of their volunteer efforts.

- **May 1995:** Newman receives the 1995 James Beard Humanitarian of the Year Award in the annual gala celebration in New York City. The award honors a person who has made significant progress to help humanity by developing programs and/or molding ideas and attitudes on helping those less fortunate through efforts within the food and beverage industry.

- **June 1995:** Situated thirty-five miles outside of Paris, near Fontainebleau, on three hundred acres of fields and woods, L'Envol becomes the newest member camp.

- **October 1996:** Newman awards over $300,000 in charity prizes to the winners of the Sixth Annual Newman's Own and *Good Housekeeping* Recipe Contest. The contest perseveres despite a fire at the contest venue, Rockefeller Center.

- **November 1996:** "Say Cheese" (Five Cheese Pasta Sauce) joins Newman's line of all-natural pasta sauces, featuring five cheeses— blue, Parmesan, Romano, Asiago, and provolone—in a base of fresh tomatoes, white wine, and extra-virgin olive oil.

- **December 1996:** Balsamic Vinaigrette Salad Dressing features a blend of canola oil and extra-virgin olive oil, plus the distinct taste of aged balsamic vinegar.

- **June 1997:** Newman's Own products are now distributed internationally to Japan, Canada, Hong Kong, France, Germany, Scandinavia, Iceland, and Brazil, with factories in England and Australia.

- **January 1998:** Newman's Own Steak Sauce is introduced with the tag line: "Preferred by 9 out of 10 cows . . . we'll steak our reputation on it." The gang at Newman's Own is attempting to convert the tenth cow. Parisienne Dijon Lime Salad Dressing is introduced with the warning: "May produce unexpected romantic results."

- **January 1999:** Newman's Own debuts the "dressing that united

Italy"—new Family Recipe Italian—a vinaigrette with Romano cheese.

- **April 1999:** Paul Newman responds to the earthquake disaster in Kosovo by donating $250,000 to aid victims.
- **June 2000:** The Association of Hole in the Wall Camps is founded to serve as an umbrella organization uniting the family of Hole in the Wall Gang Camps.
- **April 2000:** Paul Newman teams up with Oprah Winfrey and Jeff Bezos of Amazon in the "Use Your Life" Awards, a yearlong national charity partnership that identifies and supports innovative grassroots charities with $50,000. Newman donates $600,000 through this partnership.
- **January 2001:** Parmesan & Roasted Garlic Dressing is introduced—the dressing that commemorates the ill-starred lovers Prince Romeo Parmesano and Lady Julietta Garlico.
- **June 2001:** Paul Newman and Ford Motor Company partner with America's Second Harvest to fight hunger in rural America. Together they donate fourteen trucks (filled with Newman's Own products) to rural food banks.
- **April 2002:** Newman's Own introduces three new salad dressings: new Two Thousand Island (twice the islands of any other brand), Parmesiano Italiano, and Red Wine Vinegar & Olive Oil.
- **2002:** Under Newman's leadership, the Association of Hole in the Wall Gang Camps begins a pilot program in partnership with Okavango Wilderness Safaris and Mokolodi Nature Reserve, to provide a camp experience for children affected with HIV/AIDS in Botswana and Namibia.
- **December 2002:** Newman's Own posts record results for charity in 2002—sales of $109 million and profits of $12.3 million, with charity donations now totaling $137 million.

- **Spring 2004:** The Painted Turtle Camp to open in Lake Hughes, California.
- **Summer 2004:** The Victory Junction Gang Camp to open in Randleman, North Carolina.
- **2005:** The Jordan River Village, a special camp for special children, will be built in the north of Israel overlooking the Sea of Galilee. This will be the first permanent site in the Middle East designed specifically for children suffering from life-threatening and chronic diseases.

THE ASSOCIATION OF HITWG CAMPS, INC.
SUPPORT DATA—2002
LISTING OF STATES AND COUNTRIES SERVED:

BOGGY CREEK GANG CAMP
EUSTIS, FL:
- District of Columbia
- Florida
- Georgia
- Maine
- Mississippi
- New Jersey
- New York
- North Carolina
- Pennsylvania
- Utah
- Wisconsin

DOUBLE H HOLE IN THE
WOODS RANCH
LAKE LUZERNE, NY:
- Connecticut
- Delaware
- Florida
- Indiana
- Maine
- Massachusetts
- New Hampshire
- New Jersey
- New York
- Pennsylvania
- Tennessee
- Vermont

Canada
Switzerland

L'ENVOL
FRANCE:
- France
- Luxembourg
- Spain

THE HOLE IN THE WALL
GANG CAMP
ASHFORD, CT:
- Arizona
- Colorado
- Connecticut
- Delaware
- District of Columbia
- Florida
- Georgia
- Illinois
- Kansas
- Maine
- Maryland
- Massachusetts
- Michigan
- Minnesota
- North Carolina
- New Hampshire
- New Jersey

New York
Ohio
Oklahoma
Oregon
Pennsylvania
Rhode Island
South Dakota
Tennessee
Texas
Virginia
West Virginia

Canada
Germany
Ireland
United Kingdom

Denmark
Finland
Germany
Greece
Hungary
Iceland
Ireland
Norway
Poland
Portugal
Republic of Georgia
Russia
Spain
Sweden
Switzerland
United Kingdom
USA

BARRETSTOWN GANG CAMP

IRELAND:
Austria
Belarus
Cyprus
Czech Republic

AFRICA PROGRAMS:
Botswana
South Africa
Tanzania
Zambia

*Association camps serve children
in 31 different states (USA)
and 28 countries.*

BOGGY CREEK GANG CAMP
EUSTIS, FL:
Asthma
Cancer
Craniofacial *(retreats only)*
Diabetes *(retreats only)*
Epilepsy
Heart/cardiovascular disease
Hemophilia
HIV/AIDS
Kidney disease
Rheumatic disease
Sickle-cell anemia
Spina bifida *(retreats only)*
Disorders requiring ventilator
    assistance *(retreats only)*

DOUBLE H HOLE IN THE
WOODS RANCH
LAKE LUZERNE, NY:
Cancer
Leukemia
Sickle-cell anemia
Hemophilia
HIV/AIDS
Neuromuscular disorders
    (i.e., CP, MD, spina bifida,
    arthrogryposis)
Thalassemia
Other blood disorders

Ataxia-telangiectasia
Congenital heart disease
Gaucher's disease
ITP
Von Willebrand's disease

THE HOLE IN THE WALL
GANG CAMP
ASHFORD, CT:
Cancer
Sickle-cell anemia
HIV/AIDS
Hemophilia
Thalassemia
Other blood-related illnesses
"Orphan diseases" (e.g.,
    mucopolysaccharidoses)

BARRETSTOWN GANG CAMP
IRELAND:
Cancer
Hematology-related diseases
    Anemia
    Thalassemia
    Hemophilia
Renal-related diseases
    (including transplants)
Immunodeficiency diseases
HIV/AIDS
IGG, IGA deficiency

L'ENVOL POUR LES ENFANTS
  EUROPEENS
FRANCE:
  Leukemia
  Solid tumors
  Lymphoma
  HIV/AIDS
  Sickle-cell anemia
  Congenital immunodeficiency
  Diabetes
  Cystic fibrosis
  Connectivites (ACJ, LED)
  Digestive system disease
    (Crohn's disease)
  Hemophilia

Prader-Willi syndrome
Phacomatoses (Weber,
  Bourneville, Hausen)
Metabolic disease (PCU,
  glycogenosis)
Thalassemia
Kidney deficiency,
  nephropathy
Hepatitis, liver grafts
Heart defects
Other blood diseases (aplasia)
Transplant
Genetic disease
Others

*Over 30 different
disease groups are serviced.*

FROM

THE CAMPERS

My name is Mallory Cyr. I've been at The Hole in the Wall for seven years. I'm 16 years old. My sister Maisy and I have an extremely rare digestive disorder called Microvillous Inclusion Disease. Our mom explains it like this: the little tiny hairs on the little tiny hairs in the intestine—otherwise known as the microvilli—are ingrown. This causes us to not digest food properly, so we have to get our daily nutrition over a 12-hour period through a direct line into our bloodstreams.

As any normal kid would, I always wanted to go to a real overnight summer camp, but none was willing to be responsible for such intense, unfamiliar medical care. To protect our permanent IV lines, we need to use special dressings to take showers and go swimming, and the dressing must be changed after every shower or swim. All the special-medical-needs camps were limited to cancer or diabetes. Finally after telling my mother I wanted to have cancer so I could go to camp, we discovered the indescribable, abnormally wonderful place called "The Hole in the Wall Gang Camp."

There were sooo many wonderful people at the camp that I felt like I was part of a giant family! I was glad there were nurses to help do the medical tasks so that I would feel like I was at home. I was able to trust them with all my medical needs. I knew they would always do the right thing!

Going to camp has made me realize that I was not the only one with an illness and that it's not something you need to hide but merely accept as part of you. Camp has also given me the chance to climb a 35-foot climbing wall and to sign my name at the top right next to my parents' signatures, from when they climbed on a Parents' Weekend. This summer when I climbed the wall for the last time as a camper I was not only able to write a final note to my parents, but I wrote one to my little sister Maisy who will climb the wall in a few years. It is such an emotional experience, looking down and seeing all the people who just helped you get to the top, and seeing notes and signatures from people who have made it to the top already and shared the same experience. I always cry when I get there.

• • •

The mentality of a child growing up with hemophilia is possibly one of the most misunderstood aspects of the disease. Teachers, concerned parents, family friends and relatives are constantly being reminded and remindful of the supposed limitations of hemophilia. All I wanted growing up was to be a normal kid. However, my desire to be normal wasn't really a desire at all. I simply forgot I had hemophilia. When a limitation or obstacle presented itself in my life, I simply found a way around, over or straight through it.

By the time I had reached my teenage years, I had virtually forgotten the fact that I was limited by hemophilia. Bleeds, long hospital trips and pain had been integrated into my life and forgotten about. In my entire life, I can think of only one experience in which I have positively embraced hemophilia, come to terms with the disease and met other people like me in a positive environment. This experience is the way in which I hope in the future to give back to the hemophilia community.

Summer camp at the Hole in the Wall was the most positive hemophilia-related experience in my life. Camp introduced me to other kids with bleeding disorders, and gave us an environment to interact and to together defy our limitation. There were never real discussions about our common ailment; it was through activities and interaction that we were able to come to terms with it, and realize that there were no limitations that we could not overcome. Camp was definitely one of the most positive experiences of my life.

I sincerely hope and plan to devote many summers in my future to volunteering at one of the camps. Many of the counselors and volunteers there had an extremely positive influence on my life, to this very day. While I was unconsciously burying hemophilia at home, these people helped me to deal with it and still succeed. I hope that I can influence and help other hemophiliacs as I was helped.

—THOMAS RUSSOMANO

• • •

I can't begin to tell you how thankful I am that you let me into camp. People used the phrase "I had the time of my life" but you really haven't until you've gone to camp—it really was the time of my life. I've been sick for four and one half years and going to camp last year was the greatest opportunity of my life. It was wonderful being with other people who took pills every day and had an occasional IV, we had a lot in common. Another thing about camp is that I felt safe and free. At first I was a little shaky about staying away from home for a week, but after the first day, I felt like it *was* home. Being at camp was like being in a world where nothing was wrong and I was as free as a bird, and THAT is a GREAT feeling. What you did for me and all the other campers was the greatest thing that anybody has ever done and right now I am the most thankful person in the world. I love you all.

—KATIE GRENNEN

• • •

My name is Kelly Foy and my fight against cancer began when I was seven years old. I was diagnosed with Acute Lymphoblastic Leukemia. I'd been pale, bruising easily, and experiencing temperatures.

The summer before I finished treatment in October of 1999 was my first year at the Hole in the Wall Gang Camp. It was great! The counselors were awesome and they treated me like I was part of their family. In 2000, I enjoyed my second year at camp. I had the time of my life that year.

In May of 2001, I found out that I had relapsed. I was not looking forward to more years of hospital stays and IV drips. I think I was more depressed for that period of time in my life than ever. And then the application for Camp came and I felt a joy in my heart that I hadn't felt in a while. I had my fingers and toes crossed hoping I would get in. I did! There was a point in the week when I got a temperature and the nurses gave me all the necessary meds that I needed, but I still had to be transported to the hospital for extra care. Before I left, Kevin, the arts and crafts counselor, had painted a Scooby-Blue dog on my head (I was bald from chemo). Fortunately, I was well enough to return to Camp for the last couple of days of the session, and when I got back everyone treated me like nothing had happened. I fit right back in. And even though I was not feeling too well and was very lethargic, I still had a really awesome time.

A year ago in September of 2001, I had a bone marrow transplant, but I was able to return to Camp for my fourth time this past summer, and once again I had the time of my life. Because of the transplant I had some restrictions, but the counselors didn't let that stop me from having a good time.

The Hole in the Wall has been my second home and I could never imagine not ever going. Camp was that relief I needed after having needles stuck in my arms for days at a time. Camp is the best thing that's happened to me throughout this whole unbelievable journey with the fight against cancer.

•   •   •

My name is Jordan Mann. I was diagnosed with bone cancer in 1997, when I was 8 years old. I had to have treatments of chemotherapy and many surgeries. I had surgeries in my right hip and my right leg. The worst part of cancer is staying in the hospital away from your friends and family. The only good part about the hospital was meeting lots of new people—one of those people told me about Hole in the Wall.

My first summer here I was still in the middle of chemo, I was bald and I was using crutches. When my mom came to pick me up on the last day, my crutches had been painted all different colors by Sherry, the Camp Artist. After camp, when I'd go to the hospital with my crutches, people would know it was me and that I was a camp person. If I didn't have my crutches, they sometimes didn't recognize me—I was just another bald kid at the hospital.

Camp means a lot to me because it's so fun—I love going to the Woodshop, Arts and Crafts, the Creative Zone. I love the people and the staff. One time when I was having a bad night and I missed my mom, my counselor took me outside to the cabin circle to talk and look at the night sky. We saw a shooting star. I knew that God had sent me that shooting star, and also my counselor, to let me know that everything was all right.

It's a very bad thing to have cancer, but it's just a part of life and you've gotta be confident and try to get through. Camp is one of the things that have allowed me to do that.

· · ·

As I look back over my life I see many years of joy and pain. Both shine through like the sun. In my opinion, pain has had the biggest effect on my life. My trials have made me a better person inside and out. Pain over the years took over my mind and body. It made me feel there wasn't a thing I could do and that I was the only person who felt that way. Every day of my life I felt this way until the Hole in the Wall Gang Camp came into my life. It has been the light in my darkness, my music in my time of silence, my outlet in the maze of life, my joy in my time of sorrow, my rainbow after the rain, my memory of yesterday and dream of tomorrow. This camp has changed my life forever and will always be a part of me. I've learned so many valuable lessons while being here and learning of others' experiences. Some of them have been . . . live every day to the fullest, and friends are like diamonds, precious and rare, cherish and love them, then begin to share. One day I hope to come back and be a counselor here. I want to give back that part of me the camp gave to me, so that others may have a piece of it too.

—TESHA FRANCES FRAZIER

•   •   •

My name is Alyssa Wise. When I turned 13 on December 27, 2000, I thought I had everything going for me: a 4.0 grade point average, dancing 12 hours each week and competing on my dance team. My social schedule was full of the typical weekend activities of movies, shopping and sleepovers with my friends.

That winter, I started feeling tired and worn out. Everyone told my Mom that teenagers sleep a lot, but she knew there had to be something more. We were in and out of the pediatrician's office with fevers and other flu-like symptoms, but they just thought I had some kind of virus. I had always been one of the strongest and most physically fit dancers on my team, but I was barely able to complete a 3-minute number without having breathing problems.

After several weeks of tests, I received a confirmed diagnosis from the oncologist: Stage IV, nodular sclerosis, Hodgkin's Lymphoma. I had a mass that took up a third of my chest and bent my esophagus, as well as having hundreds of tiny tumors spread throughout my lungs. It was worse than we expected, and Dr. Emami said I had been sick for a very long time.

The next few visits to the hospital were scary, to say the least, but I told myself that I had to maintain a positive attitude. Because of the advanced stage of my cancer, high doses of very potent chemotherapy were used. I was on an intense treatment cycle that barely gave my body any time to recover before starting the next round of chemo. The hospital was my home away from home.

After months of treatment, I was declared officially cancer-free on February 6, 2002! It was a great feeling, but also very scary. I wondered what would happen if the cancer came back.

During one of my follow-up appointments, Lisa, the oncology social worker, asked me if I would be interested in attending the Hole in the Wall Gang Camp. I jumped at the opportunity!

When I arrived at camp I could hardly believe how neat it was, how friendly and outgoing everyone was. I met amazing kids who have overcome challenging obstacles that most kids will never have to face. It was great to let loose, have fun, and feel like I could forget my illness, even if it was only for a week. Although they say time flies when you're having fun, it seemed like the days at Hole in the Wall lasted forever.

I believe those who have experienced the battle with life-threatening illnesses know the meaning of living life to the fullest, and value each and every day. Because of some of the side effects of my treatment, my legs haven't been strong enough for me to begin Pointe classes, and I still have to take meds to deal with the side effects of the chemo. But at least I am alive and can walk. I have discovered that true friends love you even when you are bald and puffed up from medication. I am also closer to my family because of all we have been through together. I've thought a lot about what I want to do with my life, and I know it will involve something that lets me help people because I have been inspired by all the people who have helped me.

I can't wait to come back to Camp next year!

• • •

"Your child has cancer" are the most devastating words you can hear as the parent of a young child. Last fall, three weeks into the first grade school year, my daughter Caroline was diagnosed with acute lymphoblastic leukemia. At that point, I knew we were about to begin the fight of our lives. The world as we knew it was completely over. Gone were the days of any normal routine. No more violin lessons, choir practices or soccer games. No more playmates after school—or even school itself. No more planning weekends out of town or fitting a quick trip to the grocery store into the jam-packed daily schedule. The familiar daily routines even seemed frivolous as my attentions focused into a new mode—a mode of survival.

Like most parents of young children, I had always looked into the eyes of my child and seen the future—bright and full of hopes and dreams yet to be realized. Immediately after her diagnosis, I was terrified to look deep into Caroline's eyes. I was too uncertain of the possible reflection's change.

Throughout the treatment process, I have met some amazing children, who like Caroline have been robbed of a typical childhood. These children have taught me a tremendous respect for life and its precious fragility. The determination and resiliency these children possess is overwhelming. They may be fighting for their lives, but they are still children wanting all of the things which other children want.

Their dreams are real and their eyes <u>still</u> look bravely into the future—and it is bright and filled with promise. Only with these children there are a few twists and turns. There are no guarantees.

This year has been a very humbling experience for me personally. Caroline is responding so well to her treatment—but I've met so many other children who have not—several of whom have lost their battle with cancer. These children taught me about a whole new world—not one based on pity and despair—but one based on courage. I am sure that you too, in working with these children, have seen their strength, their hope and their amazing respect for each other as they fight their individual battles. Their lives have been molded by cancer. It ironically makes them strong and mature way beyond their years. Their victories need celebrating and their struggles need acknowledgment. This is exactly what your camp gives them. Celebration. Acknowledgment. Acceptance. No questions asked.

My belief in angels has expanded as I've met some strong candidates for halos in this past year. I can assure you that you've certainly earned your wings. The gift of life and *living* which you have generously given to each camper fortunate enough to be with you is such a magical gift and, like the wood fairy, will live forever in these children's dreams.

—CINDY WOFFORD

CARTOONS

OUR EATERS

WRITE

Dear P. Brigando Newman;

   Recently after reading about some of the research on hot spicy foods by Irwin Ziment, M.D., as to lung congestion and sinus problems, which I suffer from, I decided to try some of your salsa sauce. I now eat your salsa several times per week and have experienced a clearing of the lung congestion that has troubled me for years. Doctor Ziment was correct in his advice. As a seventy-four year old man with a heart condition, when I went to bed at night if I turned on my left side I was conscious of the congestion in my lungs. It was amazing the results after a few days of eating cheese and crackers topped with your salsa, my left lung is now clear as a bell.

   Good luck and thanks for a great product, both appetizing and a potent medicine.

                    Sincerely yours,

                    J.B.

                    Delanson, NY

Dear Mr. Newman:

Thank you for a sock it to 'em spaghetti sauce that people can enjoy naked. Our culture has a difficult time separating nakedness from sexuality. It is entirely possible to be very sexual and have clothes on. Also possible is to be naked and not registering sexual feelings from it.

Many families live here all year. Other families visit over holidays or during the summer. There is no sexual activity allowed outside of your accommodation. Offenders will be asked to keep loving to hugs and kisses and no fondling in front of others.

I felt that you might be interested in another segment of spaghetti society that enjoy romance and living to the fullest.

C.D.
Fargo, ND

Dear Mr. Newman:

For a very long time I wanted to send you this letter, to let you know that your delicious "Paul Newman" Dressing is a household item in our home since it came to the market. As a matter of fact, this is the only salad dressing we use. Even my husband, who fell into a coma 4 years ago and never recovered, raises his eyebrows when I feed him your dressing, that's how much he likes it. Well, you sure made a family happy, and I want to congratulate you for it.

Fondly,

G.G.

Plano, TX

Dear Sirs,

I am writing you this letter in regards to Newman's Own Virgin Lemonade. I am an auctioneer and on occasion while working my throat will get dry and have phlegm in it and makes me get hoarse. When the above happens and I get hoarse, nothing else will cut this phlegm and dryness except this Virgin Lemonade. It cuts through and cleans right up my hoarseness. You should put it on the bottle—cuts through phlegm.

Thank you very much,

L.E., Cortland, NY

To Newman and Hotchner:

I am a very old lady and thought I was beyond any possibilities of titillation until I literally stumbled over a bottle of Newman's Own Olive Oil and Vinegar Dressing.

Beaucoup insouciance! Threw away my trifocals and enlisted in a defunct health club.

Eternally yours,
J.D.
Sacramento, CA

Dear Sirs,

First off, I loved "The Sting". Secondly, do you still make the "Bandito Diablo" sauce? I really like it. One day, however, it just wasn't there anymore. I liked "The Hustler" but "The Color of Money" wasn't so good. One time when I spent the night in jail I told the jailer that I could eat 50 hard-boiled eggs. He said to shut up. I bet Paul doesn't like Richard Dreyfuss. I bet no one does.

Your pal,
M.E.
Portland, OR

Dear Mr. Newman:

I am 13 years old and I find that I really enjoy your Olive Oil and Vinegar Dressing. It doesn't make my mom have heartburn like other dressings we have tried, doesn't give me a stomachache, and doesn't give my father the squirts. My father, Ed, said that he finds that he doesn't go to the bathroom as much as he did before. All this is true, you have to believe me, I'm not lying.

Paul Newman
Newman's Own
Westport, CT

S. B.
East Windsor, NJ

Dear Paul,

I am a 67-year-old Nun (Sister of Mercy) who has been in love with you for about 30 years, although I must admit to a brief infatuation with Dan Rather.

I'm writing to ask you to consider a donation from the proceeds from your delicious dressings, sauces, and popcorn to our high school in Savannah, GA—Saint Vincent's Academy.

I'll be praying and awaiting your positive response. I know you won't cut me off with nothing (the way Dan did Connie)!

Sincerely,
Sister B.W.
Savannah, GA

G.M.

Dear Paul,

I have found the way to get through the Safeway check out line thanks to you here in San Francisco.

I had picked up a jar of your Sockarooni Sauce for some Crab Cioppino. Well, I am reading the label while standing in line and I start to crack up. Next thing every one moves over to other lines–it was like Moses parting the sea!

So thank you,

G.M.

San Francisco, CA

SAN FRANCISCO, CA

Dear Mr. Newman:

My name is Marci. I am having my pet human
being type you this thank you letter. Last
night my human fixed himself some pasta with
your sauce for the first time. As usual I
only get the leftovers but wow! My human
having eyes bigger than his brain had
prepared himself way too much. In fact so
much extra that I got an entire plate full.
It was the best sauce I have ever had. I
started eating, first I licked off all
the sauce. Then I ate all of the pasta.
I couldn't quit. It was the cat's meow.
Oh, forgive me.

> Thanks again,
> Marci
> Dover, DE

P.S. Could you maybe come out with a sauce
with a little ground mouse or bird in it?
No, probably the FDA wouldn't like that.

Dear Mr. Newman,

I really like your spaghetti sauce. My mom buys it all the time. Especially your sock it to em sauce. Do you need a very nice tabby mouser cat for your factory to chase any stray mice that might wander in? Or if you don't need one at your factory do you need one at home? This is sort of an emergency so please answer the letter fast. Also my mother wants to know if you cook at home or does your wife.

Thank you very much.

Sincerely,

H.W., Round Hill, VA

Dear Paul:

While dumpster-diving at Vons I found a case of your pasta sauce in which one jar had broken messing up the rest and the whole flat thrown away. I considered just taking a couple of the cleanest ones, seeing that it was cheese flavored & probably pretty obnoxious because of it. But I took them all, cleaned them up and, lo these many weeks, have enjoyed. The last jar as good as the first, let me tell you. What a blessing.

Thank you.

D.D.

Bishop, CA

Dear Robert Redford,

Hi. My name is Mookie. I am 12 years old and like you a lot. Will you send me your picture?

I love your salad dressing. I sometimes drink it with ice cubes in it. It's better than you'd think. Have you ever thought of making roasting chickens and then dehydrate them so people can make them at home just by adding water? I know I'd buy it. Write me if you want more ideas. People say I'm a creative genius (even though I had to repeat the 6th grade-oh well. Are you smart? Were you a good student?

Bye.

M.L., Bethesda, MD

Newman's Own—
Good Housekeeping
Magazine
Winning Recipes

CHICKEN CASSIDY KEBABS
AND SUNDANCE ORZO PILAF

FOR CHICKEN CASSIDY KEBABS

**2 pounds boneless, skinless chicken breasts,
cut into 2-inch cubes or pieces**

FOR THE MARINADE

1 cup Newman's Own Olive Oil and Vinegar Dressing

2 teaspoons fresh gingerroot, ground into paste

2 teaspoons fresh garlic paste

³/₄ teaspoon cayenne pepper (less if desired)

FOR SUNDANCE ORZO PILAF

**3 cups freshly cooked orzo (1¹/₃ cups uncooked,
prepared according to package directions)**

1 cup Newman's Own Olive Oil and Vinegar Dressing

¹/₃ cup orange juice concentrate

¹/₂ cup minced mint

2 tablespoons red chili oil (less if desired)

1 teaspoon minced gingerroot

¹/₂ cup chopped dried apricots

1 cup currants

1 cup slivered almonds, toasted

1 cup sun dried tomatoes in oil, chopped

1 large green pepper, seeded and diced

1 cup minced red onion

1 cup cubed goat cheese (optional)

Thin orange slices for garnish

Mint sprigs for garnish

Place the chicken in a glass dish or nonreactive bowl. Mix the marinade ingredients together and pour over the chicken, turning to coat well. Cover the dish and refrigerate for at least 5 hours or overnight, turning occasionally. Soak 12 wooden skewers in water for 15 minutes. Remove the chicken from the marinade and thread onto the soaked wooden skewers. Set aside.

To make the pilaf: Place the orzo in a large bowl. In a separate bowl whisk together the salad dressing, orange juice concentrate, mint, chili oil, and ginger. Pour the dressing over the orzo and mix well. Add the remaining ingredients and toss gently. Cover the bowl and keep at room temperature while the kebabs are cooking.

Preheat the grill or broiler. When ready to serve, grill or broil skewers for about 5 to 6 minutes on each side.

Transfer the orzo to a serving tray. Arrange the cooked chicken skewers attractively on top. Garnish with the orange slices and mint sprigs.

CORNMEAL SQUARES WITH SALSA

1 cup yellow cornmeal

1 teaspoon chili powder

4 cups water

1 teaspoon salt

1 cup (4 ounces) grated Monterey Jack cheese

One 4-ounce can green chilies, drained, chopped, and patted dry

$^1/_4$ cup chopped fresh cilantro

6 tablespoons vegetable oil

One 11-ounce jar Newman's Own Chunky Salsa (mild, medium, or hot)

Oil a 15 x 10 x ½-inch baking pan.

Combine the cornmeal and chili powder in a small bowl. Set aside.

In a large saucepan, bring the water and salt to a boil over medium heat. Sprinkle the cornmeal mixture, ¼ cup at a time, into the water, whisking constantly. Cook, stirring constantly with a wooden spoon, until thickened, about 10 minutes. Stir in the cheese, chilies, and cilantro. Spread the batter evenly in the prepared pan. Refrigerate until cooled completely.

Cut the cooked cornmeal into fifteen 3 x 3¼-inch squares. In a large, non-stick saucepan, heat 2 tablespoons of the oil over medium-high heat. Place 5 squares in the skillet and cook, turning once, until golden brown, about 8 to 10 minutes. Remove to a plate.

Cook the remaining squares, in batches of 5, in the same manner, with the remaining oil.

Serve warm topped with the salsa.

CHICKEN WITH ORANGE-SALSA BUTTER

**4 tablespoons unsalted butter,
at room temperature**

**4 tablespoons Newman's Own Chunky Bandito Salsa
(mild, medium, or hot)**

1 teaspoon grated orange zest

$^1/_2$ cup flour

$^1/_2$ teaspoon salt

$^1/_4$ teaspoon cayenne pepper

4 boneless, skinless chicken breast halves

$^1/_4$ cup fresh orange juice

2 tablespoons vegetable oil

Orange slices for garnish

In a food processor, process the butter, salsa, and orange zest until smooth. Spoon the butter onto a sheet of plastic wrap and shape into a log. Wrap tightly and freeze.

Combine the flour, salt, and cayenne pepper on a plate.

Dip the chicken pieces, one at a time, in the orange juice and then in the seasoned flour; shake off the excess. Discard the juice and the flour.

Heat the oil in a large nonstick skillet over medium-high heat. Add the chicken in one layer and cook, turning once, until golden brown and cooked through, about 7 to 8 minutes depending on thickness. Place on dinner plates.

Cut the cold orange butter into 4 pieces and put a piece on each chicken breast. Garnish with orange slices and serve at once.

Blaze's Shrimp and Sausage Creole

2 tablespoons unsalted butter or margarine

2 celery stalks, chopped

1 medium yellow bell pepper, chopped

1 large yellow onion, chopped

³/₄ pound kielbasa sausage, sliced

1 clove garlic, minced

1¹/₂ cups clam juice

1 cup Newman's Own Bombolina
   (Tomato and Fresh Basil) Sauce

FOR THE SPICE MIXTURE

1 bay leaf

¹/₂ teaspoon dried thyme leaves

¹/₂ teaspoon dried basil leaves

¹/₂ teaspoon salt

¹/₂ teaspoon ground white pepper

¹/₄ teaspoon cayenne pepper

¹/₄ teaspoon ground black pepper

1 pound medium shrimp, peeled and rinsed

3 cups hot cooked rice (1 cup uncooked, prepared
   according to package directions)

In a 12-inch skillet, heat the butter or margarine over medium-high heat until hot. Add the celery and pepper, and sauté for 8 to 10 minutes, until softened. Remove the mixture from the skillet and set aside. Add the onion and kielbasa to the skillet and sauté for 10 minutes. Stir in the garlic and cook for 30 seconds.

Add the clam juice, sauce, and all the spice mixture ingredients, and bring to a boil. Cover and simmer for 5 minutes. Add the shrimp and cook for 2 to 3 minutes, until the shrimp become opaque throughout. Add the reserved celery mixture and heat through. Discard bay leaf.

To serve, spoon the hot rice into large shallow soup bowls and top with the shrimp and sausage Creole.

A Drowning Pool of Praline in a Chocolate Tart

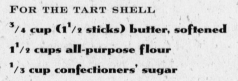

For the tart shell

$^3/_4$ cup (1$^1/_2$ sticks) butter, softened

1$^1/_2$ cups all-purpose flour

$^1/_3$ cup confectioners' sugar

For the praline-chocolate filling

Two 3-ounce bars Newman's Own Organics Chocolate (Sweet Dark Chocolate or Sweet Dark Chocolate with Orange Oil), broken into pieces

$^3/_4$ cup heavy or whipping cream

One 9$^1/_2$-ounce bag caramels, unwrapped

1$^1/_2$ cups pecans, toasted and coarsely chopped

Preheat the oven to 375°F.

Prepare the tart shell: Place all tart shell ingredients in the bowl of a food processor and pulse until they form moist crumbs. Sprinkle the crumbs in a 9-inch tart pan with a removable bottom and press the crumbs together to form a crust on the bottom and up the sides of the pan. Prick the dough all over with a fork. Line the tart shell with foil and fill with pie weights, dried beans, or uncooked rice. Bake for 25 minutes. Remove the foil and the weights and bake for another 15 to 20 minutes until golden, pressing the crust with the back of a spoon if it puffs and loosely covering any dark spots with foil.

Prepare the praline-chocolate filling: Combine the chocolate and ¼ cup of the cream in a 1-quart saucepan and place over medium-low heat. Cook gently, stirring frequently, until chocolate is melted. Set aside 2 tablespoons of the chocolate mixture. Spread the remaining chocolate mixture evenly over the bottom of the cooled tart crust. Chill the tart crust and the reserved chocolate mixture for 20 minutes.

Put the caramels and the remaining ½ cup cream in a 2-quart saucepan and place over medium-low heat. Heat until the caramels are melted and the mixture is smooth, stirring occasionally. Stir in the pecans and quickly pour the caramel over the chocolate layer in the tart pan; spread evenly.

In a small saucepan over low heat, heat the reserved chocolate mixture 1 to 2 minutes, stirring until melted, or microwave for 10 seconds. Using a fork, drizzle the chocolate in a zigzag pattern over the top of the tart. Chill at least 1 hour before serving. Store uneaten tart in the refrigerator.

LEMON MUSTARD CHICKEN

Serves 4

4 boneless, skinless chicken breast halves

**1 cup Newman's Own Old Fashioned Roadside
    Virgin Lemonade**

¹/₄ cup fresh bread crumbs

¹/₄ cup finely chopped pecans or walnuts

1 egg

5 tablespoons whole-grain mustard

Vegetable oil for frying

**3 to 4 teaspoons walnut oil or 1¹/₂ teaspoons dark
    sesame oil**

¹/₂ cup chicken broth

¹/₄ cup heavy cream

**Salt and freshly ground black pepper
    to taste**

Marinate the chicken in the lemonade for 1 hour. Drain, reserving the lemonade, and pat the chicken dry with paper towels.

Stir together the bread crumbs and nuts on a plate. Put the egg in a shallow bowl and beat lightly. Place 3 tablespoons of the mustard in another bowl.

Brush the chicken with the mustard, dip into the beaten egg, then dredge in the crumb-nut mixture. Chill, loosely covered, for 2 to 3 hours.

Heat ½ inch of the vegetable oil with the walnut oil in a large skillet until hot. Add the chicken and fry, turning once, for 10 to 12 minutes. Remove to a serving platter and keep warm.

While the chicken is cooking, combine the reserved lemonade, broth, and the remaining 2 tablespoons of the mustard in a small saucepan. Bring to a boil and reduce over high heat to ½ cup. Add the cream and cook about 1½ minutes to heat through and thicken slightly. Season with salt and pepper, and pour over the chicken. Serve hot.

Lamb Shanks Inferno

4 lamb shanks (about 3 to 4 pounds total)

Salt and freshly ground black pepper
  to taste

$^1/_4$ cup flour

6 tablespoons olive oil

1 small onion, diced

2 cloves garlic, minced

1 carrot, peeled and diced

$^3/_4$ cup dry red wine

$^3/_4$ cup beef broth

One 26-ounce jar Newman's Own
  Fra Diavolo Sauce

Parsley sprigs for garnish

Preheat the oven to 350°F.

Season the lamb shanks with salt and pepper, and dredge them in the flour; tap off the excess. Heat 5 tablespoons of the oil in a 5-quart Dutch oven until medium-hot. Add 2 of the lamb shanks, brown them all over, then remove to a plate. Repeat with the remaining 2 lamb shanks.

Scrape the brown bits off the bottom of the pan and discard. Heat the remaining 1 tablespoon of oil in the Dutch oven until medium-hot. Add the onion and garlic, and sauté until soft and translucent. Add the carrot and sauté for 1 to 2 minutes. Add the red wine, raise the heat to high, and reduce the wine by half. Add the beef broth and sauce, and bring just to a boil. Immediately remove the pan from the heat.

Add the lamb shanks to the Dutch oven, spoon the sauce over them, and cover tightly. Bake for 2 hours, or until the meat is fork-tender.

Remove the shanks from the sauce and keep them warm. Skim the fat from the sauce. Adjust the seasonings.

Serve the lamb shanks with the sauce and garnish with the parsley sprigs.

LEMONADE TORTE FOR A LONG HOT SUMMER

Serves 8

recipes

³/₄ cup blanched almonds

1¹/₂ cups sugar

1¹/₂ cups whole-wheat bread crumbs

¹/₄ teaspoon baking powder

¹/₄ teaspoon ground cinnamon

1 tablespoon grated lemon peel

6 large egg whites

1 cup Newman's Own Old Fashioned Roadside
   Virgin Lemonade

2 tablespoons confectioners' sugar

Position a rack in the lower third of the oven. Preheat the oven to 350°F. Butter and flour a 9-inch springform pan.

In a food processor, grind the almonds with 1 cup of the sugar. In a medium bowl, mix the ground almond mixture with the bread crumbs, baking powder, cinnamon, and lemon peel. Set aside.

In a large bowl, beat the egg whites and the remaining ½ cup sugar with an electric mixer on high speed until stiff peaks form. Gently fold the crumb mixture into the beaten egg whites. Pour the mixture into the prepared springform pan and bake on the lower oven rack for 1 hour.

Meanwhile, put the lemonade in a saucepan over medium-high heat, and cook until reduced by half, about 10 minutes.

Remove the torte from the oven. Pour the reduced lemonade gradually over the top of the hot torte. Let the torte stand in the pan on a wire rack until cool.

To serve, remove the sides of the springform pan and dust the top of the torte with confectioners' sugar.

NEWMAN'S OWN POPCORN TRAIL MIX

Serves 12 (makes about 12 cups)

One 3.5-ounce bag Newman's Own
  Microwave Popcorn, natural flavor
1 cup dry roasted salted peanuts
$^1/_2$ cup raisins
$^1/_2$ cup chopped dried apricots
$^1/_3$ cup sunflower seeds
$^1/_2$ cup firmly packed brown sugar
$^1/_4$ cup butter
2 tablespoons honey
$^1/_4$ teaspoon salt
$^1/_4$ teaspoon baking soda

Preheat the oven to 350°F. Grease a 14 x 10-inch metal baking pan.

Pop the microwave popcorn according to package directions. Pour the popcorn into a large bowl. Add the peanuts, raisins, apricots, and sunflower seeds. Mix well. Set aside.

In a 1-quart glass measuring cup, mix the brown sugar, butter, honey, and salt. Microwave, uncovered, on high for 90 seconds. Stir well. Continue microwaving on high for 30 seconds. The mixture should be boiling. Continue boiling for 90 seconds. Remove the mixture from the microwave and stir in the baking soda. Pour the syrup mixture over the popcorn, stirring until mixed.

Place the mixture into the greased pan. Bake 15 minutes, stirring once. Remove from the oven to cool and crisp. Store in a tightly covered container.

LASAGNA PRIMAVERA

One 8-ounce package lasagna noodles

3 carrots, cut into $^1/_4$-inch slices

1 cup broccoli florets

1 cup zucchini slices, cut $^1/_4$ inch thick

1 crookneck squash, cut into $^1/_4$-inch slices

Two 10-ounce packages frozen chopped spinach, thawed

8 ounces ricotta cheese

One 26-ounce jar Newman's Own Marinara Sauce
** with Mushrooms or Newman's Own Bombolina**
** (Tomato and Fresh Basil) Sauce**

12 ounces shredded mozzarella cheese

$^1/_2$ cup grated Parmesan cheese

Preheat the oven to 400°F. Line a 15 x 10-inch baking sheet with foil.

Bring 3 quarts of water to a boil in a 6-quart saucepan over high heat.
Add the lasagna noodles. Cook for 5 minutes. Add the carrots. Cook
2 minutes more. Add the broccoli, zucchini, and crookneck squash
and cook for 2 minutes more or until the pasta is tender. Drain well.

Squeeze liquid from the spinach. Combine the spinach with the ricotta
cheese. Spread ⅓ of the marinara sauce in the bottom of a 3-quart
rectangular baking pan. Line the pan with half of the lasagna noodles.
Top with half of each vegetable, half of the spinach mixture, and half
of the mozzarella cheese. Pour half of the remaining sauce over the
top. Repeat these layers, ending with the remaining sauce. Sprinkle
the Parmesan cheese over the sauce.

Bake the lasagna, uncovered, on the prepared baking sheet for about
30 minutes, or until hot in the center. Let stand for 10 minutes before
serving.

The lasagna may be prepared up to 2 days before baking and kept,
covered, in the refrigerator. If made in advance and chilled, bake for
1 hour at 350°F.

SANTA FE CHICKEN AND
POTATO SALAD

**One 8-ounce bottle Newman's Own Family
  Recipe Italian Salad Dressing**

**One 11-ounce jar Newman's Own Chunky Salsa
  (mild, medium, or hot)**

4 boneless, skinless chicken breast halves

8 small new potatoes or 4 medium potatoes

$^1/_4$ cup water

**4 cups assorted salad greens, such as leaf lettuce,
  spinach, radicchio, endive, etc., washed, dried,
  and torn into bite-size pieces**

$^1/_2$ large red onion, thinly sliced

**One 15$^1/_4$-ounce can red kidney beans, rinsed
  and drained**

1 red pepper, thinly sliced

1 yellow pepper, thinly sliced

In a medium bowl, combine the salad dressing and the salsa. Place
the chicken breasts in a glass dish or sealable plastic bag. Pour over
½ cup of the dressing-salsa mixture, turning the chicken to coat
well. Cover the dish or seal the bag and let marinate in the refrigerator
for 1½ to 2 hours. Reserve the remaining dressing-salsa mixture.

Place the potatoes in a 2-quart microwave-safe dish with the water. Microwave on high 8 to 10 minutes or until tender; drain and set aside.

Preheat the grill or broiler. Grill or broil the chicken breasts on medium
heat for 6 to 7 minutes per side.

While grilling, assemble the salad greens on 4 dinner plates. Slice the
warm potatoes and chicken. Divide evenly among the plates the
potatoes, chicken, kidney beans, onions, and peppers.

Warm the dressing-salsa mixture in the microwave for 1 to 2 minutes.
Drizzle over the salads and serve immediately.

ACKNOWLEDGMENTS

With apologies to those we have probably overlooked we thank the following for helping us out:

Robert Forrester, Andy Crowley, Jimmy Canton, Karen Allen, Max Yurenda, Edward Salzano, David Kalman, Claire Panke, Darice Worth, Mike Havard, Mary Harper, Kirsten McKamy, Roberta Pearson, Kerry Goldstein, Tom Indoe, and Virginia Riser.

We are especially indebted to Timothy Hotchner for the skillful and illuminating interviews he filmed.

We also appreciate the support and encouragement of Doubleday's Stephen Rubin, and the editing cooperation of Lorna Owen.

As for our editor and publisher, Nan Talese, we take special note of her bravery, dexterity, and exquisite patience and permissiveness in dealing with the authors.

CREDITS

Grateful acknowledgment is made to the following for permission to reprint the cartoons in this book:

The New Yorker: © The New Yorker Collection 1983 Arnie Levin from cartoonbank.com. All rights reserved.

Off the Mark: Cartoon copyrighted by Mark Parisim, printed with permission.

Out of Bounds: Reprinted with the special permission of Kind Features Syndicate.

B.C.: By permission of John L. Hart FLP, and Creators Syndicate, Inc.

Sylvia: © Nicole Hollander 1987. Printed with permission.

Conrad: Copyright, Tribune Media Services, Inc. All Rights Reserved. Reprinted with permission.

Blue-Eyed Peas: © Scott Masear

Title page photograph and photographs on part opening pages are copyright © S. D. Colhoun.

Paul Newman (known as ol' PL to both friends and enemies): The "L" stands for "Leonard" or "Lunkhead." He answers to both. He is probably best known for his spectacularly successful food conglomerate. In addition to giving the profits to charity, he also ran Frank Sinatra out of the spaghetti sauce business. On the downside, the spaghetti sauce is outgrossing his films. He did graduate from Kenyon College magna cum lager and in the process begat a laundry business, which was the only student-run enterprise on Main Street. Yale University later awarded him an Honorary Doctorate of Humane Letters for unknown reasons. He has won four Sports Car Club of America National Championships and is listed in the *Guinness Book of World Records* as the oldest driver (70) to win a professionally sanctioned race (24 Hours of Daytona, 1995). He is married to the best actress on the planet, was number 19 on Nixon's enemies list, and purely by accident has fifty-one films and four Broadway plays to his credit. He is generally considered by professionals to be the worst fisherman on the East Coast.

A. E. Hotchner fully intended to be a career lawyer, but after two stultifying years practicing with a St. Louis law firm, he escaped into the wild blue yonder of the Air Force, vowing never to look at another Corpus Juris Secundum. After the war, Hotch became a literary bounty hunter, and in the process met Ernest Hemingway, with whom he buddied around for fourteen years, an adventurous period that Hotch chronicled in *Papa Hemingway*, which was published in thirty-four countries in twenty-eight different languages. In between selling salad dressing, Hotch has written fifteen books, a dozen plays and musicals, and scores of television dramas. In 1999, Washington University conferred on him an honorary Doctor of Letters to go along with his Doctor of Law degree, but he is proudest of the fact that he was crowned marbles champion of St. Louis when he was in the sixth grade.